"This book is more than an expression of thoughts and motivational messages, it is an absolute reflection of the author sharing his entrepreneurial passion and his commitment to excellence—all the while grounded by his immense spirituality and dedication to treating all that he encounters in work and life as family. I am honored and blessed that the author's philosophy brought prosperity and value to my own business, but more importantly, helped me to find a new friend and inspirational mentor."

—R. Chad Perkins, MD, Chief Medical Officer,
Tri State Community Clinics

"Phil Berry's essays are equal parts powerful, accessible, actionable, and motivational. He tells stories to which we can relate and that resonate deeply. *Every Day is Game Day* offers simple, tangible examples of how the choices we make every day can ultimately define our perspectives, our happiness and our ability to achieve our true potential."

—Kristina Graff, Executive Director, Timmy Global Health

"In *Every Day is Game Day*, Phil captures the essence of what is important to live our best lives each day. Most people wait for some mythical date, i.e., retirement, graduation, new job, children grow up, etc., when they plan to start living their best lives. Phil, through his detailed roadmap in the book, shows us how to stop where we are and start to live today our best lives ever!"

—Wanda Johnson, CEO, Preempt Corp.

"Phil Berry is a mentor and friend. He has a gift for asking the right question and for expanding perspectives. In *Every Day is Game Day*, Phil generously shares stories and reflections that we can all learn from and apply at work and in life."

—Emily C. Krueger, COO, 16 Tech

"This book is for the individual, the team member, the entrepreneur, and those searching for clarity for living. Phil's style is very accessible, down-to-earth, filled with insightful common-sense thinking and peppered with wise quotes from a variety of authors, playwrights, sports figures and others. Read in short spurts, it will inspire deeper reflection."

—Rev. Richard Ginther, Pastor,
Our Lady of Lourdes Catholic Church

"Phil Berry's book is amazing and should really resonate with all readers. The essays provide strength for anyone going through anything challenging. I see myself, family members, and friends in the stories and they all provide purpose and meaning to things in life that not many authors touch on. This book provides a road map that is easily followed to improve one's life and the decisions we make. I would highly recommend this book for anyone trying to find peace and motivation for this thing we call life and to walk through life with a purpose."

—Bobby J. Long – President & CEO, Longevity Consulting, LLC.

EVERY DAY

YOUR LIFE. YOUR GAME. YOUR CHOICE.

IS GAME DAY

EVERY DAY
YOUR LIFE. YOUR GAME. YOUR CHOICE.
IS GAME DAY

PHILLIP BERRY

CROSS
STONE
press

Indianapolis, Indiana

Editor: Jon VanZile
Interior Design: Ghislain Viau
Cover Design: Kevin Craig
Cover Photo: Phillip Berry
Author Photo: Jessica Bishop
Content Curation: Madison Choiniere

Do Your Best

Do your best.
Her parting words hung in the air,
and my mind,
as I fumbled through the dark.

The night was heavy upon us
and her words seemed to flow
from another world, not fitting the moment
yet profoundly prescient.

The nature and definition
of a person's best is ephemeral,
changing, wraithlike with the moment
there and gone silently.

These words were encouragement.
A prayer for a troubled heart
and an admonishment
to a challenged soul.

Earlier that day, I spoke of adversity
as a single obstacle.
She reminded me of its true nature
as an enduring companion.

I paused in the silence of the night.
Considering her words as I walked to the door.
In the hazy, half-awake moment,
I felt the compassion, and forgiveness.

You are not alone.
You don't have to be perfect.
We will find a way.
Do your best.

p.g. berry

To Sally: 30 years later, you're still showing up. Where you go, is where I want to be.

Contents

SECTION ONE
Show Up Every Day

SECTION TWO
Own It Every Day

SECTION THREE
Stand for Something Every Day

SECTION FOUR
Choose Happiness Every Day

SECTION FIVE
Give Your Best Every Day

SECTION SIX
Be Vulnerable Every Day

SECTION SEVEN
Every Day Is Game Day

Foreword

By Madison Choiniere

I am part of the 1 percent. Part of the lucky few who have experienced game day in the competitive arena of college basketball. Nothing compared to the thrill and challenge of performing on the court, and nothing was as bittersweet as the day it was over. Game day has long been associated with only the chosen who participate in athletics, but my dad challenges this way of thinking by bringing game day to our every day lives. The season of intense competition has passed for me, but the joy of game day can be found in the ordinary.

There are unique associations that accompany game day. These include readiness, determination, perseverance, and grit. These are valuable characteristics that should be lived out in every moment of our lives. My dad invites us to do just that. Through his own personal experience on the battlefield of business and life, he carves a way for each of us to step up to the plate and start aiming for the stars. In this series of essays, he guides and challenges our approach to the game of life. He reminds us that in the midst of adversity and struggle we can learn to shift our focus to one of gratitude. We can still choose to show up and do our best no matter the circumstances.

These lessons have been intimately woven into my life as I've had the pleasure of observing and learning from my dad for twenty-four years as his daughter. You see, we go way back to the day I was born. It was from that moment that he began molding and leading me. He's always had a knack for turning my athletic struggles into important life lessons. He's shown me the joy of showing up each day and putting my best foot forward. He is a living example of hard work and determination turned into success. Knowing him as I do, his lessons are especially important to me. I see the deep character he's built over the years, and I see a person worth emulating. I especially admire the intense joy he finds in showing up for game day. His life is a beautiful reminder of finding the beauty amongst the adversity.

Game day is fun, it's something I always used to look forward to as an athlete. It was an opportunity to compete with my team, work hard, get better, and lose myself in the sport I loved. But game day shouldn't be reserved for athletes alone and it isn't. Each morning that we wake up we have a choice to make. Let this book guide you as you make the decision to compete, work hard, get better, and get lost in the pursuit of your passions. Nothing feels better then a battle well fought and character well formed.

Introduction

In 1997, I accepted a promotion within the high-growth IT services company where I worked and we moved to the Chicago area. It was an exciting transition. A new job, a new city, and the company had recently been bought by a telecom giant to serve as the platform for a move into consulting services.

Six months into the new position, I found myself on the phone with my dad, telling him how much I was struggling.

Why was I struggling? It wasn't the move. My family loved our new life in Naperville, Illinois. It wasn't the company. In spite of the acquisition, we were pretty much left alone and viewed as very strategic within our new corporate structure. It wasn't the money. At twenty-eight years old, I was making more than I had ever made, heading a branch operation with more than thirty team members. My chief complaint? I was bored.

My dad listened patiently as I described my struggle to get motivated for my days and my desire for more responsibility. He heard of my challenges with customers and the competitive marketplace. He listened to me talk enviously about one of my peers whose branch was double the size of my branch (as was his income). He endured my whining for nearly an hour before he smiled (I could hear it in his voice) and said, "Phillip, I don't feel sorry for you." He paused for a moment as I absorbed his comment and then continued. "I don't feel sorry for you, because you are in the game. Every day, you get up and have another opportunity to play. You can swing for the fences or simply try to get a base hit, but you are still in the game. I would have done anything to have the opportunities before you."

Fast forward fifteen years and I'm talking with my oldest daughter as she struggles to adjust to her first semester in college, where she is playing basketball on a scholarship. She is describing the brutal practices, an unsympathetic coach, and the impossible challenges of balancing schoolwork with everything else. Suddenly, I hear my dad's voice in my head as I find myself telling her that she's "in the game" and that "I would have done anything to be able to play basketball in college."

For me, my dad's comment was a reminder. It was an anchor to a point in time. Perhaps I just needed someone to sympathize with my challenges for a while. Maybe I wanted him to tell me that everything would be alright. His call to gratitude and to taking a different perspective on the challenges, and opportunities, of my situation were timely. Though my daughter didn't need me to tell her how amazing I thought her accomplishments were, she did need me to help her see the bigger picture amid the adversity.

You see, every day is game day. We all wake up with opportunities on the horizon. We all walk into our days with new possibilities, new challenges, and the chance to be our best. We are living the infinite game and winning is simply the opportunity to do it again the next day. The circumstances will change, but our opportunity to be all of which we are capable remains.

Don't like the game you're in? Pick a new game. Tired of not getting enough playing time? Find another team, or better yet, improve your skills. In this game, there is a position for everyone and we set the measures of our own success. To play it well, you must answer two questions: What is my best? How do I strive for it every day?

Though I can't answer those questions for you, I can tell you that you'll know when you're there. Find your game. Play your game. Be your best. Every day.

Show Up Every Day

Your days are finite, and they pass quickly. Every morning you awake, you have a chance to make a difference. Be present for that opportunity. Show up every day.

Your Life, Your Game

Each day, we awaken with the opportunity to win the game of our life. Sometimes it is literally an athletic contest—sports are very much a part of our culture. But more often, our games are nondescript encounters with our own possibilities. Generally, no one is keeping score. Occasionally, we can clearly tell if we won or lost. Usually, the contests pass unnoticed.

Games typically involve a winner and a loser. In the game of your life, there are also winners and losers. However, I'd like to adjust our traditional definition of winning and losing. Sure, you can still show up and lose an argument, lose a deal, lose an athletic contest, or lose a loved one. Those unavoidable losses are part of life's experience. In my definition, winning and losing revolve around how you prepare, play, and react to the games of your life. Winning centers on getting as close as possible to the best version of you, every day. Losing happens when you fall short of that ideal. The powerfully compelling thing about playing your game this way is that when you are your best self, the world is a better place. Here, we can all win.

Life is a collection of games. Our own personal World Series. We win when we make a difference in the lives of those around us. We win when we are good stewards of our gifts. We win when we embrace the opportunity to keep playing.

We lose when we stop trying. We lose when we don't show up. We lose when we squander our gifts or fail to recognize them. We lose when we don't work to make life better for others. We lose when we stop loving, don't forgive, or hurt or blame others. The scoring system is easy: one point added for a win or one point deducted for a loss. Your job is to finish every day with as many points as possible. Keep score for a day. Are you winning or losing the game of your life?

"It's just a game." How many times have we used this expression to soften a loss? Our parents introduced it to us early on as a coping technique for losing. This is one reason that the game metaphor is particularly applicable to our life. Losing is part of it. I mention it because, in the game of your life, you determine if you win or lose. Not because you can avoid loss, but because you can control yourself. Your effort, attitude, preparation, generosity, and reactions are all within your scope of control. All you have to do is show up and put your gifts in motion. It's your life; it's your game. Show up every day.

Phillip Berry

Show Up for Yourself By Living in the Moment

Be happy in the moment, that's enough.
Each moment is all we need, not more.
—*Mother Teresa*

As the term "mindfulness" approaches the numbness-inducing zone of cliché, it seems appropriate to take one more look at it before it is lost in the abyss of buzzword purgatory. I'm a personal believer in the notion of mindfulness, but I was recently reminded how dangerously close I am to losing this important word as I rolled my eyes after hearing it used one time too many in a conversation.

Mindfulness is generally defined as a mental state achieved by focusing one's awareness on the present moment. I was first introduced to the concept in 1989 by Robin Williams in the movie *Dead Poets Society*. In it, Williams's character introduces the term "carpe diem," a Latin expression meaning "seize the day." About ten years later, a friend shared the phrase "living in the moment" with me and I've been a fan ever since.

To fully grasp the notion of living in the moment, it is helpful to consider the alternatives. If one is not living in the moment, she might be living in the past. Of course, she isn't literally living in the past, but she may be emotionally or intellectually tied to lost moments. And that is the rub. Living in the past suggests an inability to let go and move on.

Lost youth. Lost love. Lost opportunity. Lost moments. To live in the past is to focus on something you no longer have, often at the expense of that which is sitting right in front of you.

> To live in the past is to focus on something you no longer have, often at the expense of that which is sitting right in front of you.

Another contrast to living in the moment is living for tomorrow. To live for tomorrow is to sacrifice the present for what is to come. It is often tied to dissatisfaction with current circumstances, but it can also be tied to ambition and aspiration. Living for tomorrow is the pragmatic virtue of delayed gratification in the hope of some future gain. Traditionally, much of our society's tie to living for tomorrow stemmed from the Puritan ethic of self-discipline and thrift. In recent years, it could be argued that the concept has morphed into something different, as consumerism has created a culture of "more"—more money, more stuff, more food, more likes…always more tomorrow than today.

Finally, and most insidiously, not living in the moment is to live amid distraction. Or more precisely: to *exist* amid distraction. We are not living fully if we are allowing distractions to disrupt our moments. These distractions are so pervasive as to not require any narrative—you know exactly what I mean.

What is it to "live in the moment" or "be mindful"? Simply put, it is making the most of the moment you are in. To "seize the day" is to not miss what is in front of you as you worry about yesterday, tomorrow, or the cacophony of distractions assaulting your senses. Living in the moment isn't about a blindly idealistic vision of living for today to allay the loss of yesterday or the fear of tomorrow; it is having the faith to be fully present in this moment, trusting that you will find a way through the obstacles that will undoubtedly come.

Our role as parents is particularly conflicted as it relates to living in the moment. We struggle with the perpetual battle between our career life and our family life. This intersection is a recipe for guilt and, frequently, a sense of loss down the road as we recall experiences and moments lost. The sad thing is that, though our inner video recorder always replays the big moments lost—a child's missed performance, award ceremony, or sporting event—the bigger losses are in the moments that we are physically there but not fully present.

Professionally, we struggle as well: multitasking during meetings, half-listening to conversations, checking our phones constantly (100–150 times per day). This is a recipe for regret, a sense of loss, and missed opportunities. Mindfulness calls us to intentionally focus on the current moment in a more singular way. Living in the moment is experiencing fully that person, painting, sunset, thought, vision, music, message, word, or silence in front of you in spite of the myriad interruptions seeking to pull you away.

Buzzword or not, the concept is real. Living in the moment isn't centered on self-gratification, avoidance of responsibility, or numbness to difficulties or loss. Being present is maximizing this moment and living it fully. What are you doing to live in the moment, be mindful, and seize the day? Are you holding onto something that is limiting your ability to be present? Are you looking toward something that is lessening what you are giving to today? Are you allowing noise to be an obstacle to fully experiencing the gifts standing before you? If so, stop it. *Now.* Be intentional. Be mindful. Be present. Live fully in this moment. It is the ultimate gift to your future self.

The Gift of Showing Up for Others

Showing up begins long before you stand at the start. Prove yourself an exception in a world where people talk more than act. Intent without follow-through is hollow. Disappoint yourself enough times and empty is how you feel. Make yourself proud. Fill yourself up. Show up.
—Gina Greenlee, *Postcards and Pearls:*
Life Lessons from Solo Moments on the Road

In our world of 24/7 news, tweets, posts, pins, pics, email, video, and podcasts, it has become increasingly difficult to get anyone's attention. The deluge of information is exacerbated by a media-induced ADD that has caused us to consume content in soundbites, 120 characters, clips, and snippets. Traditional news outlets complained of this fact in the recent election by pointing out that people can now choose a source of information based on what it communicates, regardless of the quality of reporting, and effectively tune out all other noise. Of course, people have always chosen their preferred source of information—but the point is that everyone with a Twitter handle (about 317 million active this quarter) has become a source of information. The volumes are truly staggering.

Part of the spectacle of social media revolves around friends, followers, and fans. We build our following to give and receive information. Much of the interaction in our circles revolves around likes, retweets, and shares. It would seem that our contact points are growing, and we are now connected to so many more than we would have been otherwise. Or are we?

I suppose a like or follow might be construed as a connection, but a curious thing has happened as our networks have grown: we've reduced our interactions to button-clicking on posts and shares, often without even digging any further than the headline. As easy as these mediums make it to interact with one another, they are really more of a platform for blasting our voice, image, or product into an increasingly disinterested world. As our networks have grown, our circles have contracted.

Sure, people may comment. But who is commenting? There are two types: your immediate circle, which has a deeper connection with you, or the broader world that may happen to see

> ## As our networks have grown, our circles have contracted.

something you post and will typically only react if it irritates them. Granted, there are many different levels of "quality" in our social media networks. Some networks have a strong community based on shared interests. Many are looser connections. To further complicate the situation, posts and shares get moved along the information superhighway to others who may or may not notice, like, or share but still register as a view, giving us the mysterious "impression" we see referenced in social media ad bundles. Is five thousand views good? Perhaps.

A side-effect of this circus of information overload is that it has gotten increasingly difficult to get people to "show up." I use this term very broadly to describe how we engage with others. It can be seen in all types of interactions: potential transactions, requests for information, efforts to entertain, cries for help, offers to share, invitations to participate, and on and on and on. Let me provide some examples:

- **Hiring**. Over the last year, we've posted about a dozen positions. Each position has had great response—people submitting resumes expressing interest. Our single biggest challenge with hiring? Getting people to show up for the interview. Yes, those who have accepted invitations to physically interview simply don't show. This cycle has repeated itself at an alarming rate.

- **Buying**. Over the last twelve months, we've had a number of projects within our companies for which we needed to purchase a product or help from another company. These projects ranged from construction to equipment to consulting. It has been staggering how incredibly unresponsive vendors have been to requests for information or efforts to purchase from them. In some cases, we've seen similar issues to the hiring issue, in which suppliers simply don't show for appointments to sell or do work. One might argue that they must be so busy that they can't do any more work, but I think there is something else going on. I think it is a combination of information overload, the capacity to manage it, and possibly a lack of motivation.

- **Inviting**. Throughout the year, we hold numerous events ranging from informational to social to launch-type events. Traditionally, we would mail physical invitations to prospective attendees. As time has gone on, the norm has evolved to emailed invitations and then promotion via social media. We generally get a good response, but I'm always surprised at the number of people who simply don't respond. In many cases, non-responders are folks who I thought had stronger connections to our company or people. Are they not seeing the invitations, posts, tweets, and shares? Or is it just another data point that appears on the horizon and disappears as quickly?

There is power in responding, in showing up. It is a gift. Yes, there has always been a continuum of folks who show up or not in varying degrees. The sad thing is that it has become easier than ever to show up, acknowledge, and engage with other human beings, and yet so often we don't. We no longer have any excuses. We are a click, like, share, email, or retweet away from telling someone else that we noticed. We don't even have to talk with them. We don't even have to dial a number.

Now, look at who is showing up for you. That is your circle. Those are the people who give a hoot about anything happening in your life. You know of whom I speak. They are the ones who are there whether they need you or not. They are the ones who want to see you succeed. They are the ones who like, share, retweet, or simply respond when asked. What about the rest of us? No, we can't be intimate with everyone. We can't engage in the same way with each person in our network. But can we do better? Can we show up just a little more when asked? If we can't, then perhaps we need to consider why we remain a friend or follower and what we expect of those who friend or follow us.

To Truly Be Present, Cultivate Your Awareness

If, then, I were asked for the most important advice I could give, that which I considered to be the most useful to the men of our century, I should simply say: in the name of God, stop a moment, cease your work, look around you.

—Leo Tolstoy, *Essays, Letters and Miscellanies*

A trip to Costco provided a fascinating opportunity to observe others in a state counter to mindfulness. I was not in a hurry and only needed a couple of things, so I grabbed my cart and casually headed toward my first stop in the back of the store. As I moved through the store, I was repeatedly cut off in a variety of places. A mom and her two children cut across my path to get some snacks from a sample vendor. A man with glasses and a blue shirt angled across my cart to get to the meat cooler. An older woman in a blue dress patterned with yellow stopped abruptly in a turn to check her phone. For me, it was a bit of a surreal trip through the store because I felt like an outsider, an observer of some bizarre dance of shoppers, clerks, and vendors.

With each interruption of my journey, I stopped and patiently (mostly) waited for the opportunity to go around or for the person to reorient him or herself and clear my path. As I watched each of them, I noticed that they had no idea I was there; I was invisible. Each person was engrossed in his/her mission or distraction. My presence was irrelevant. All of them were completely unaware of me and pretty much everyone else around them.

The experience reminded me of a scene in the 1999 science fiction thriller, *The Matrix*. In it, Neo (the hero) learns that his real body is in fact plugged into a computer and his entire life has been a virtual journey within the program called the Matrix. In one scene, Neo is placed into a virtual reality training program to show him how the Matrix works. His mind is transported to a crowded New York sidewalk, and as he walks, he is bumped and pushed by people from all sides. They are oblivious to him, and he is hardly able to proceed on the sidewalk because of all the people. Beside him, his mentor, Morpheus, is moving fluidly within the same crowd—no bumps, no pushing—he is navigating the crowd effortlessly. The lesson is that Morpheus understands how the Matrix works and this allows him to navigate the crowd without disruption.

As I considered the bumps and interruptions at Costco, I realized that my reaction to them placed the responsibility on the other person. The other person cut me off. The other person blocked my path. These were disruptions to me because I expected something different. How would my experience have been different if I had expected them to behave as if they were unaware of me? In this case, I would have anticipated being cut off or stopped in the aisle. It seems that Morpheus's lesson to Neo also applies to us: understanding how the system works enables you to navigate it.

Now, let's move from navigating among those who are unaware to cultivating our own awareness. The people I encountered at Costco weren't bad people, and though you might argue that their lack of awareness could be called rude, they had no intention to be discourteous. They were unaware of me and everyone else around them as they focused on their own world. We all do this. When we drive, we text or check the radio or talk on the phone. When we watch TV, we tune out the rest of this world as we escape to an alternate universe. In our offices, we half-listen to others as we are trying to get an email finished or complete a task while fooling ourselves into thinking that we're multitasking effectively. We all live some portion of our life within the world of the unaware.

On that day at Costco, I was tuned-in and really aware. Most likely, that was an exception—who knows how many people I've cut off in my years as a distracted shopper? How do we improve our awareness? In most cases, our lack of awareness is simply a bad habit. We chase the shiny objects of our life and get lost in the pursuit. The good news is that we all have powerful engines for concentration and focus that allow us to zero in on priorities when we choose. Our challenge is to be intentional in our awareness.

My suggestion for being more aware is to fully engage your senses:

- **Look** at others around you. I mean really *look* at them. When we see the details of another person, we engage at a different level. What color were his eyes? What was she wearing? When you take a moment to read facial expressions or look beyond the cursory, you will find yourself stepping to a higher level of awareness. Our powers of sight connect us in unique ways that not only increase our awareness, they also send clear signals to others. One note of caution: don't be creepy about it!

- **Listen** to the sounds of the world in which you are walking. What are people saying? Is there music playing? In our day-to-day existence, it is easy for us to drown out individual sounds in the cacophony of noise that assaults us. At Costco, I can't say that the sounds were melodic, however, I did notice the conversations and experienced some specific sounds as they related to the moving of products and calls across the speaker system. Listening in the moment made me very aware.

- **Smell** the variety of odors wafting across your path. Smell is not one of my stronger senses, but even a Costco offers up some intriguing possibilities. I noticed the sample vendors and their little grills with sausages or veggie patties. The bakery was alive with treats, and I even noticed a pleasant perfume along one aisle. Smell can be a powerful tool for engaging with your environment and building awareness.

- **Touch** when it is appropriate to touch. At Costco, I touched products and some food samples. I brushed the hand of one of the clerks as I was checking out and passing items onto the conveyor. Touch is a powerfully connective sense and engages your awareness exponentially. Touch brings acknowledgment and encouragement in a truly personal way.

Now, think about engaging your senses where you work, where you live, and where you play. Focusing your senses brings you to a heightened awareness and bonds you to your environment in a special way. When you intentionally engage your senses, you are powerfully aligning your physical presence with your mental presence. This focus allows you to connect with those around you and enables you to enjoy the benefits of full awareness. When was the last time you really thought about one or more of your senses? How did it make you feel?

The next time you are navigating around the obliviousness of another, work on your own awareness. Be fully present by bringing all of your senses to bear. My guess is that you'll find renewed satisfaction in the process and a refreshing level of connection with those around you.

Own It Every Day

Today is your day. You won't see it again. You can let the world tell you how to spend it or you can choose a direction for yourself. Carpe diem...seize the day. Own it every day.

Spark Your Own Renaissance

While I thought that I was learning how to live,
I have been learning how to die.
—Leonardo da Vinci

The Renaissance was a period of time beginning in the fourteenth century that saw a great revival of art, literature, and learning in Europe and marked the transition from the medieval to the modern world. Though there are many views on how and why this shift occurred, the Renaissance reflected a renewal in scholarly thinking, art, and culture across the continent.

The word "renaissance" means a renewal of life, vigor, and interest. It comes from the French word "renaistre," which means to be born again. It is a rebirth. Often, we go through a period of self-assessment and renewal as we enter a new year. Why wait?

What is renewal? It is a call to an earlier time. A period that captured our imagination, our energy, and our hope. Of course, renewal isn't about reliving a

> Renewal is a spiritual return to a previous moment in which, looking ahead, we felt that there was still much before us.

specific time in the past, it is about the *spirit* **of another time. Tapping into feelings and motivations**, finding the joy that was kindled in former possibilities and moments. Renewal is a spiritual return to a previous moment in which, looking ahead, we felt there was still much before us.

Another element of renaissance is rebirth. Rebirth isn't about returning—it is about beginning again. Recreating our world in a new light, with new ideas and fresh possibilities. To be reborn is to recreate ourselves in the reflection of our current capabilities, but with an eye toward our potential. Starting anew isn't throwing everything out and starting over or relinquishing the gifts that brought us to where we are. Rebirth is launching from this moment into the ones yet to be with a new sense of the possible and the will to make it real.

Where to begin? Sparking a renaissance in your life will require you to tap into the spirit of renewal and walk with intention toward the possible, a quest that is both emotional and intellectual. Here are some ideas for instigating your own renaissance:

1. Invest yourself in your renaissance.

2. Open yourself to the inspirational.

3. Shift your thinking about the present.

4. Inventory the good.

5. Map the aspirational.

6. Steel your resolve with action.

7. Set the station.

Invest Yourself in Your Renaissance

The first step is straightforward: simply decide to intentionally walk the path to your own renaissance. Once you've decided, commit to the process by setting aside time to focus on each step. To focus on your renaissance process, set a deadline and carve out thirty to forty-five minutes a day from now through your deadline. Most people won't commit. Most people won't follow through. Renaissance is about doing things differently—start with the commitment.

Then just do it. Two to three weeks of commitment to thinking about your future. Just a few minutes a day. Resolve to put in the difficult work of thinking and dreaming about what is possible. Invest your time. Invest in a notebook. Invest in a space. Invest your heart. Choose to believe that you can and will embrace renewal for your year ahead.

Open Yourself to the Inspirational

For me, reading or listening to books is an effective trigger. However, there are now so many sources of great inspiration: videos, podcasts, people. Open yourself up by reading, listening, or watching something that inspires you. I often turn to poetry. It sits outside of my day-to-day. Good poetry takes me somewhere else. The point is to get into a frame of mind and spirit that allows you to think clearly about non-urgent, less-than-concrete elements of your own life. Opening your time alone with your own form of meditation or devotion clears the baggage and inspires clarity of thinking.

Shift Your Thinking About the Present

The best way to shift your thinking is to introduce new ideas and concepts. I find that it is nearly impossible not to inspire possibility thinking when I absorb new information. Books, podcasts, and videos once again play a critical part. Now that you have opened yourself, feed your mind and heart with fresh notions. Challenge your brain with great thinking from other people. I have a collection of go-to authors who help me see myself and my world in new ways. Sometimes I turn to business-related content, and sometimes I travel farther afield and explore spiritual or philosophical material. Often, I find historical books helpful, particularly biographies.

The reality is that most of us want the bullet points, the cliff notes, the soundbites. To shift your thinking, you will need to dig deeper and force yourself to consider new ideas, other perspectives, and the world beyond the trail you walk every day. In this process, you will build a new framework within which you might create new context for you own life.

Inventory the Good

Your own renaissance will be best sparked by building on the foundation you've created for your life. Grab your notebook and dedicate a few pages to the good and the beautiful in your life. List everything you can think of: your personal gifts, the wonderful people around you, your neighborhood or city, your education, your faith, your country, your pets...all of it. This list accomplishes two things: it creates a spirit of gratitude within you, and it inventories your assets. The positive energy of gratitude, coupled with a list of what you have on your side, provides a powerful spring into the aspirational.

Map the Aspirational

Of course, I mean map *that which is* aspirational. Call it what you will: goals, objectives, possibilities, resolutions, aspirations, etc. Get that notebook back out and compile a list of aspirations. Next month, next year, the year beyond, five years...whatever. Mapping the aspirational is about looking forward and considering the possible in the context of your desires. It might make sense to break these down into categories: personal, professional, family, spiritual, etc. Your renaissance begins with where you want to go, who you want to become, and ultimately boils down to becoming the best version of yourself. What is the best version of yourself? You've opened yourself up to inspiration, you've considered other people's great ideas, you've taken an inventory of your gifts, and now you begin to consider what you are called to be, who you want to be, and how you might start down that path.

One suggestion: don't be shy. Put it out there. Stretch. What would happen if _____? Often, you'll uncover things you don't like about your life. Great! Renaissance is rebirth, and change is in the wind. When you renew and recreate, you give yourself permission to remove things that no longer fit, don't align, and/or poorly reflect the best version of yourself. Frequently, we look externally. Resist the temptation. Changing relationships, jobs, homes, cars, clothes, et al., rarely addresses the real issue until we've aligned our self with the values, gifts, priorities, and possibilities that define us. Map the aspirational by looking forward to the best version of yourself and what that means for your life.

Steel Your Resolve with Action

Forgive me for using the "A" word, but it is *absolutely* necessary. Without action, all your inspiration and aspiration will amount to little more than a slight adrenaline blip in a particular moment. To spark your renaissance, you'll need to act, again and again and again. Of course, this means taking definite steps to actualize your aspirational map. Action could be as simple as eating to match your health goals, taking a class in a foreign language, learning to play the piano, putting a new resume together—or it could be a set of long-term objectives like going back to school, sailing around the world, going to all of your child's school events for the next ten years, taking your mom to breakfast every Friday morning, etc.

The great news about action is that it feeds itself. Action creates momentum, and momentum reinforces our sense of progress. With momentum, action steels our resolve because we see it working and ultimately taking us toward our aspirations. One word of caution: don't overcomplicate this process. Take small steps. Sometimes we jump too grandly into a direction and lose our resolve in the midst of overwhelming scope. The other side of this issue is waiting for the perfect time. There is no perfect time. When you wait for the perfect time, you are simply giving yourself permission to do nothing. Sometimes, we need to steel our resolve by jumping in without perfect information, perfect timing, or perfect readiness. One of the most powerful motivators is necessity. When you commit yourself to a direction based on an action, you often trigger the necessity engine and your most resourceful self.

Set the Station

None of what I've described above is a one-time event. The reality is that we should always be in some state of renaissance for it is through the process of renewal that we grow. So, set the station. Program this channel into your routine so you can return to it daily. Revisit it when you hesitate. Revisit it when you fail. Revisit it when you lose hope. Revisit it when you doubt. Make it a part of your toolkit that you use to repair, modify, and affirm all that you are and all that you might be.

The Day Before Us

Here we are. Another day is before us. We have all been granted amazing gifts, free will, and possibility. They are ours to shepherd and nourish, or ours to squander. The responsibility is staggering. What will you do with it? How will you spend it? In the days ahead, trigger your own renaissance by resolving to be more, to do more, and aspire to more. Then commit to becoming the best version of yourself with intention and persistent effort. Who knows? You may just surprise yourself and those around you with a spark that truly makes a difference.

What Will It Be?

The object of a New Year is not that we should have a new year. It is that we should have a new soul and a new nose; new feet, a new backbone, new ears, and new eyes. Unless a particular man made New Year resolutions, he would make no resolutions. Unless a man starts afresh about things, he will certainly do nothing effective.
—G.K. Chesterton

It's 5:41 am. The house is quiet, and it is dark outside. I awoke this morning with a number of thoughts on my mind and the sense of possibility with this new day. Time will march on today, and tomorrow it begins again.

And there it is, the word "begins." When you consider it, "begins" is a simple word laden with complex implications and expectations. To begin is to start: it suggests something new, something not yet done. We tend to wrestle with endings, but we usually embrace beginnings. Why not embrace your beginning every day?

Rolling out of bed today, one question kept racing through my

"We can choose to distract ourselves with the broad, macro-level movements, trends, hopes, and fears of the greater world, or we can focus on the six inches in front of our face."

head: what will it be? A new beginning lays before us. I'm not talking about a political, social, or organizational beginning—I'll let the pundits speculate and argue about what is ahead for us in those categories.

The real question is: what will today be for us as individuals? We can choose to distract ourselves with the broad, macro-level movements, trends, hopes, and fears of the greater world, or we can focus on the six inches in front of our face. The scary, intimidating, soul-wrenching six inches that we can actually impact.

So, what will it be?

- Will it be a day of health and wellness or one of excuses?

- Will it be a day of uninspired effort or one of initiative and hope?

- Will it be a day of hiding behind excuses or one of confronting our demons?

- Will it be a day of seizing the day(s) or one of floating along on a paddle-less boat?

- Will it be a day of kindness or one of criticism?

- Will it be a day of moving forward or one of falling behind?

- Will it be a day of self-improvement or one of self-indifference?

- Will it be a day of accountability or one of blame?

- Will it be a day of possibility or one of impossibility?

- Will it be a day of dreams or one of nightmares?

- Will it be a day of helplessness or one of resolve?

- Will it be a day of grit or one of floundering?

- Will it be a day of prosperity or one of struggle?

- Will it be a day of love or a year of hate?

- Will it be a day of making a difference or one of not really mattering?

It is easy to lose ourselves in the machinations of the greater universe. It is easy to become frustrated, hopeless, and angry with what everyone else is doing or not doing. We focus on countries fighting, terrorists terrorizing, politicians lying, and people doing all sorts of things over which we have no control. As maddening as these things may be, the real challenge we face is what we choose to do in our own life. What good we choose to bring to this crazy world and how we choose to live within it.

We give ourselves permission to relinquish responsibility for something when we have absolutely no control over it—it is effortless. The hard work happens at home, in those dark, quiet moments when the noise of the outside world is nowhere to be heard. When the only voice is the one inside our head and the only choices are ones we can make. Resolution? Yes, this is where it begins. There is that word again: begin.

As you walk through today and start into tomorrow, consider your own life and the lives of those in your immediate world. Then ask yourself: what will today be for me? Then resolve to be better, for yourself and for those you love. Take a step into the frightening six inches where you own it and determine to make it a day worth remembering. We're all counting on you.

See Your Possibilities with Expansive Thinking

One of the greatest disservices we do to ourselves is to sell our ourselves short. We think narrowly about our "ities": possibilities, opportunities, and capabilities. It is easy to do. We're reminded daily of the "why nots." As small business owners, we tend to see the world in terms of our current products, markets, and revenue streams. As employees, we see our career in terms of what our current company may or may not offer. Often, we limit ourselves with incorrect assumptions about the possibilities within an existing role or organization. As spouses, siblings, friends, and associates, we continually define our world within the context of what has been and remain hesitant to truly embrace what might be.

Why do we do this? Consider a few reasons:

- **Experience has taught us**. Skinned knees and bloody noses have taught us what happens when we push ourselves too far. Failure has an acute impact on our ability to dream and an even greater impact on our willingness to execute on those dreams.

- **People remind us**. We all have friends and loved ones who remind us of past failures: ours or someone else's. Most of the world is incredibly good at finding the problem with something: bad ideas, risks, holes, gaps, poor grammar, and misspelled words. It is far easier to edit another's idea than to originate your own.

- **Instinct**. Our instincts tend to lean toward the negative or self-protective. There is good reason for this: survival. We are built to survive and have numerous internal safety features to help us achieve this mission. The problem is that surviving is not necessarily thriving, and we are built to achieve so much more.

- **We allow ourselves**. The biggest reason we think narrowly is because we allow it. We allow all of the external noise, messaging, and criticism to hold us back or convince us of what is not possible. Or, more insidiously, of what *we* are capable.

I have seen this frequently when mentoring business owners and entrepreneurs. As a society, we often envision these mavericks as having larger-than-life ambitions, goals, and visions. Quite frequently, they see themselves within the self-limiting context of today: people, money, facilities, markets, etc. Yes, there are visionaries out there building castles in the sky long before they build them on the ground, but the vast majority of entrepreneurs are actually selling themselves short every single day. The problem is that these business owners are too busy listening to the noise rather than focusing on the way forward. The noise is always much louder.

I believe the answer is to embrace expansive thinking. Thinking expansively is about focusing on the possibilities. It is asking "what if?" When we think expansively, we open our self to the universe and become receptive to a scope and expanse far beyond what lies before our eyes. This is not always easy. You may ask yourself: "How can I think expansively when I'm trying to cover payroll or a mortgage or tuition? How do I think big when I'm struggling to keep up with my workload, projects, or customer demands? When things are breaking? When people are leaving?" And on and on and on.

Thinking expansively is about being intentional with your possibilities. It is about developing a habit of seeing beyond your immediate world. It is looking for opportunities and embracing them before you have all of the answers. Expansive thinking requires you to intentionally open yourself to a world beyond you, seek pathways to that future, and walk deliberately toward those new options. I'm not suggesting that it is being foolish with your time, money, or resources. However, you need to remember that we are naturally wired to protect all of the above. It feels much less natural to push your envelope than to play it safe.

Another way to consider the idea of expansive thinking is to contrast it with focus. Common wisdom today tells us to focus, to specialize. The deeper we are with a set of skills, knowledge, and experience, the more successful we will be. Focus *is* important when seeking to achieve your objectives. The problem is that we often narrow ourselves unnecessarily in our quest to be a specialist. As human beings, we are not machines. Our mind is an infinitely curious, flexible, and receptive instrument with wide-ranging capabilities and interests. Expansive thinking calls us to bring the wide-ranging capabilities of our mind to bear on our own lives and seek all that is possible.

Embracing expansive thinking can be difficult. Here are some ideas for fostering it continuously in your life:

- **Say yes more than you say no.** Our natural state is to say no. When we say yes, we open ourselves to the universe and all of its possibilities. Find reasons to say yes and you will move toward a more naturally expansive state of mind.

- **Surround yourself with possibility people.** We all have friends, peers, and loved ones who are quite capable of reminding us of what is not possible. Find people who are believers in your possibilities, even if they don't see their own yet. Eventually, you'll help them see their own as well.

- **Collect ideas.** Ideas come to us from all places at all times. Don't ignore them. Write them down no matter how silly they are.

Each idea is a sign, a signal of some possibility. Often, ideas don't make sense in isolation, but a collection of them might present the opportunity for you to connect the dots of a bigger concept.

- **Be a consumer of information.** Find sources of new information and fresh ideas. Video, audio, and the written word present incredible opportunities to be inspired with new ideas, new concepts, and new ways of thinking. Find sources that force you to think and push you to look at things differently.

- **Experiment.** Frequently, we kill an idea at inception because it is clearly not a good concept. Thinking expansively is to consider all ideas and their potential implications. Sometimes, we need to trial an idea to see where it leads. Even if the original idea doesn't work, walking down the path often yields new discoveries.

- **Discuss ideas.** For most of us, it is incredibly difficult to sit before a blank sheet of paper and capture a collection of brilliant ideas. However, get us in a group and things start happening. Group discussions help us think expansively by bringing fuel to the idea engine and getting others involved. It is difficult not to think expansively in such situations. A word of caution: re-read the second bullet above.

Ultimately, thinking expansively is about changing your state of mind. Get out of the habit of telling yourself no before you've even started. Occasionally embrace new possibilities without clear objectives and the journey will reveal more than you expected. Form a new habit of looking beyond the obvious and you'll be rewarded with new sources of joy and fulfillment. Engage the less pragmatic visionary within you and you'll inspire yourself and those around you to new heights.

Then He Wrote, "Trump Is Going to Fix This."

Not I, nor anyone else can travel that road for you. You must travel it
by yourself. It is not far. It is within reach. Perhaps you have been
on it since you were born, and did not know. Perhaps it is everywhere—
on water and land.
—*Walt Whitman, Leaves of Grass*

This week, I received an email from a job candidate who had received a rejection notice from us. I know nothing of his story, challenges, successes, or failures. He simply submitted a resume in response to an ad and, for whatever reason, was rejected by our team with a standard form email. He felt compelled to send me an email telling me that "Trump is going to fix this." His comment stopped me in my tracks.

My first thought was a question: What is it that this individual expects Mr. Trump to fix? Did he expect Trump to improve his resume? Add years of experience to his career? Give him a collection of skills that we might find more useful? I wondered aloud, "Is he seriously typing that email to me thinking that Trump is going to give him a job?" Then it occurred to me that the tone wasn't really that hopeful; it sounded more like a desire to get even. Maybe he thought President Trump would disadvantage someone else so that he would be in a better position to secure a job.

Either way, that line of thinking is destructive to both his sense of self and his attitude toward his fellow man.

Thinking back a few years, it reminded me of another time, another election. The election of 2008 was about hope and change as well. Then it became clear: we have people waiting for someone else to fix their lives.

Where did we lose our self-reliance? When did we decide that it was someone else's fault? Why do we have citizens expecting an elected official to make their lives better?

What would I say to the individual who sent me that email? My first question would be: What are YOU doing to position YOURSELF for success? Is YOUR resume the best reflection of YOUR skills and capabilities? When YOU submitted YOUR resume, did YOU provide a cover letter telling us how YOU will bring value to our company and how YOU are the best possible candidate? Did YOU apply for a job that YOU really, really want? Did YOU research our company before applying and reference your discoveries in YOUR cover letter and YOUR resume? Did YOU discover who the hiring manger is, and did YOU make a phone call to personally introduce yourself? Do YOU think there is anything that Donald Trump, or any elected official, is going to do to address the questions above?

I love our country. I am hopeful for the future. I wish Donald Trump and all of our political leaders the very best as they lead our country toward the horizon. However, WE have got to stop waiting for someone else. WE have got to stop blaming someone else. Are there things that politicians do to make it difficult to get things done in our lives? YES! So what? That's why we have elections. After we've cast our vote, our job is to get on with the process of living as best we can.

The truth is: Donald Trump will not fix "this." Barack Obama did not fix "this." George W. Bush did not fix "this." Bill Clinton did not fix "this." And on and on and on. "This" is us. "This" is ours. Our best hope is our own effort, our own attitude, our own hope, and our own support of one another. Should we hold our elected officials accountable? Yes. Should we vote for people who align with our views? As much as we possibly can. Should we expect someone else to make our lives better? NO!

What should we do? Hope for the best. Pray for the best. Work for the best. The best that WE can possibly do and be. If all of us focus on being that best version of ourselves and giving others the best version of ourselves, we'll be far less concerned with the ebb and flow of elected officials and far more concerned with that little part of the world that we inhabit every day.

Who Will You Choose to Become?

It is our choices, Harry, that show what we truly are,
far more than our abilities.
—J.K. Rowling, Harry Potter and the Chamber of Secrets

A week ago today, my daughter, Madison, married a young man named Ryan. It was a wonderful experience for all involved. We had the opportunity to spend an entire week in Hillsdale, Michigan, making final preparations and enjoying the company of friends, family, and the community. Emotional and activity whirlwind notwithstanding, the week presented numerous opportunities for contemplation and set the stage beautifully for more than a bit of soul-searching.

Immense Decisions

In the days leading up to the ceremony, I was struck by the immensity of the decision. These two individuals are choosing to spend the rest of their lives together. They are making a vow in front of God and family that, no matter what happens, they will stand by one another for as long as they both shall live. Wow! That is commitment.

As I considered the enormity of these moments, I realized that the key here was choice. They chose each other as partners in life and, in so doing, chose a direction for their life together. Setting aside the emotionally powerful setting and spiritual element of this particular decision, there is a wonderful model here for all of us as we look forward in our own lives.

The Power of Choice

Our life is a collection of choices. The most important choice we can make is who we want to become. This isn't just a vocational choice, though we'll face that. This isn't just a geographical choice, though that may be part of it. This isn't simply a relationship choice, though relationships are certainly critical to who we become. We choose who we want to become in the minute-by-minute behaviors we exhibit that lead us a to future version of our self. Choosing who we want to become is a daily set of actions that lead to some future version of our self.

> Choosing who we want to become is a daily set of actions that lead to some future version of our self.

In the example above, Madison and Ryan have chosen a future for their lives based on a relationship commitment. They see themselves in the context of this choice and are moving intentionally in that direction—each has chosen to become something more together. From here on out, they will make daily choices that will refine and redefine their original decision. In this way, they will build a life together, but they will also be building their individual lives in the reflection of their original decision.

My first book, Stones Across the River, is about finding a path to the best version of yourself and "choice" emerges as a central element in walking that path. So often, we limit ourselves based on the choices of others: regulators, spouses, coworkers, siblings, bosses, etc. Why do we do this?

Self-Imposed Limitations

vChoosing who you want to become is the ultimate in self-empowerment. It is not being afraid to make a lifelong commitment to another human being because you know that you control the ten thousand choices that you must make during that relationship. It is choosing a certain career because you see potential and then shifting later when circumstances change. It is choosing to treat people in a certain way because your values dictate that behavior. It is choosing to say no to things that move you away from your best self and saying yes to those things that move you closer.

Along the way, we have so many opportunities to trip, pick ourselves up, and make another choice. We have the gift of a chance to course-correct, time and again. The flip side is that we are creatures of habit. Often, we tend to make similar choices over time that are defaults to patterns we reinforce again and again. This only becomes trickier as we age. Inertia is a powerful force.

So, who will you choose to become? Will you cede your power to others or to your own habits? Or will you seize those opportunities to become more? At twenty, thirty, fifty, seventy and beyond…you always have choices. Remember that previous mistakes, bad habits, the perceptions of others, or circumstances need not define your future self. What you become begins with today's choices. Choose wisely.

Stand for Something Every Day

The world is full of spectators. Observers letting others play the game as they watch. Today, you can choose to join the fray, or you can remain a spectator. Be a player. Stand for something every day.

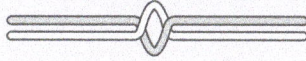

Where Do You Stand?

If you don't stand for something, you'll fall for anything.
—Alexander Hamilton

In May 2016, I had the opportunity to see Justice Clarence Thomas address the graduating class of Hillsdale College. Near the beginning of his speech, entitled, "Freedom and Obligation," Justice Thomas set the tone with this line: "I admit to being unapologetically Catholic, unapologetically patriotic, and unapologetically a constitutionalist."

Justice Thomas shared this perspective to give everyone context for the words to come. I thought it an incredibly powerful line and have rolled it around in my head many times since that day, often asking myself: "What is it to be unapologetically anything?" The very nature of the word "unapologetically" invites disagreement. It suggests an absolute position. A line in the sand. To say it exposes one to a powerful vulnerability that looks a lot like strength.

In our day-to-day work lives, where do we choose to be unapologetic? Where do we draw our lines in the sand to clearly mark where we stand? The stakes are high: a wrong position can cost you a job, a customer, an employee, a lawsuit, money, or perhaps a relationship. If you ever wonder about this, try drawing a line in the sand on Facebook or LinkedIn and watch what happens. Social media is a new highway along which we drive in vehicles called Twitter, Facebook, or LinkedIn. Just like on our physical highways, where people are incredibly bold when wrapped in two tons of steel, it is easy to confront, curse, and display appalling rudeness when one feels safe, unreachable. Choosing a position and sharing it publicly makes you vulnerable.

Where do we stand in our work lives? I'm often asked the question: "Why?" Why write? Why start a company? Why take risks? Why choose a particular industry? Why hire a particular person? Why have four children? Why get married at twenty-two? The choices we make highlight the lines we've drawn. The positions we've taken. As I look back, it is easy to see the pattern in choices I've made and my underlying worldview. It is also easy to plot the mistakes and the inflection points where my line in the sand has shifted. That is my story, and for it, I feel unapologetic.

> Choosing a position and sharing it publicly makes you vulnerable.

In a few weeks, I'll publish my first book. During the course of pulling it together and discussing it, I've discovered a new position for me: I'm unapologetically entrepreneurial. No, this isn't a religious or political line in the sand. It doesn't hold heavy social commentary and shouldn't subject me to particularly intense disagreement. My discovery is one of curious introspection as I continue on this journey. Of course, the position isn't new. It has informed and influenced my decisions for many years. To recognize it and acknowledge it is liberating. Choosing the path of unapologetically embracing anything is empowering. In the process, you give yourself permission to step into a version of yourself that aligns with something deeper. Perhaps that something deeper is one of your "Why's."

For what do you offer no apology? Your beliefs? Your art? Your job? Your family? Where do you draw that line for the things that you represent? Do you stand in that place proudly and unapologetically? Or do you keep a lower, safer profile? Being unapologetic isn't about imposing your position on another or even trying to move someone to your side of the line. It is taking a principled stand for what you believe while trusting yourself to believe something. We don't have to expose ourselves to great risks in order to stand for something. Nor do we need to shrink from the responsibility of believing in something no matter how big or small. Though it may be risky to stand for something, I think it's far riskier to stand for nothing.

So, go ahead, put it out there. Tell us where you unapologetically stand. You may surprise some people, or more likely, you may find that we suspected it all along. Either way, you'll likely release a set of inner fears tied to being discovered and finally give yourself permission to stand boldly for those foundational elements stirring within.

Business, Honor, and Integrity

*The most tragic thing in the world is a man of genius
who is not a man of honor.*
—George Bernard Shaw

I recently participated in a meeting in which an individual was pitching a new business concept. He had a novel idea to bring together several elements of a solution that could potentially impact a number of stakeholders in the process. During the course of the presentation, he suggested that certain organizations would buy into the concept even though the results were inconclusive. When I asked, "Why?" he responded that, even with inconclusive results, this approach was better than anything else available. Certain companies would buy it even though the value was questionable, and this individual was prepared to sell it knowing that truth.

I must confess to being dumbfounded. Business often gets a bad rap for dubious deals amid accusations of pillaging the unsuspecting buyer, but I have never personally experienced such a blatant example in my own journeys. My next set of statements created a moderately hostile exchange and the awkward closing of the conversation. My point? We had no interest in pursuing any venture that did not have the intent and substance to do the right thing on behalf of everyone involved in the transaction. Conversation over.

We don't hear much about honor these days, and the word "integrity" often feels like a buzzword relegated to the bucket we use to hold trite and meaningless clichés. It is unfortunate that it doesn't hold a higher place in our public discourse because it's so incredibly important to our moral fabric. Perhaps it is because we've become so accustomed to a "gray zone" of moral and ethical relativism. In a society of such intense individual liberty and diverse beliefs, we have somehow convinced ourselves that choosing to believe that something is okay actually makes it okay. How unfortunate.

The TRUTH is that it's not okay to charge someone for something that doesn't do what it purports to do. It is not okay to deceive someone on the merits of a product or service simply because one can. In most cases, these things work themselves out because, once it has been done, the buyer doesn't return. Over the long term, the law of the jungle takes care of it as we discover that one cannot build a sustainable business around hucksterism. Even so, I find it truly sad that there are those who seek this path on a transactional basis and sacrifice their honor and integrity on the altar of greed.

Our name, our honor, and our integrity should mean something in the market. Not that we are perfect but that we work to do the right thing. There are "gray zones" in the market that reflect unclear expectations, but there shouldn't be "gray zones" for ethical behavior. Even the best of intentions are sometimes mangled in the process of doing business, but what do we get when we don't even start with the best of intentions? Even when mistakes and misunderstandings occur, we can act with honor and maintain our integrity. Even when we disagree, we can do so honorably.

And there we have it: disagreement. Today, we've taken disagreement to new heights and the "wailing and gnashing of teeth" has become a national pastime. Integrity isn't just missing in our transactions. "Fake news" is the new catchphrase for gossip, supposition, presumption, and pure fiction now being pronounced as fact and discovery. Outright dishonesty or at least an incredibly casual approach to the truth has left us in a moral vacuum rationalized in the relativism of behavioral equivalence: your bad behavior justifies my bad behavior. The real danger here is that it now permeates all aspects of our society: the news we read, the posts we share, the lies we spew, as well as the snake oil we sell. When we allow our honor and integrity to slide in the small things, it is only a matter of time before it explodes in the big ones. In this place, we all lose.

Seem obvious? Apparently not. Until we as professionals demonstrate that honor is still important and that we are working to do the right thing for all our stakeholders, we will continue to see businesses vilified as raiders and pillagers. Until we as humans sharing this society demonstrate that integrity is still important, we will continue to be fed "fake news" and experience the maddening disconnect that currently plagues us. Perhaps that is the natural evolution of a society with such expansive freedoms as ours. For my part, I don't believe it has to be, and I feel that we can CHOOSE to do the right thing every time. Not to be perfect, for that will never happen, but to behave with honor and integrity.

What's Your Point?

A good speech should be like a woman's skirt; long enough to cover the subject and short enough to create interest.
—Winston S. Churchill

You've been asked to participate in a small panel discussion on topic X. The purpose of the panel is to present three perspectives on the topic and generate discussion within the panel and among the audience. As you begin to speak, your mind starts wandering. Your mouth is moving, you're looking at individuals in the audience, you're searching your brain, and before you know it, you're rambling. The simple act of sharing your view becomes a fifteen-minute journey into the depths of the inane, the banal, and the irrelevant. Your voice finally tails off into a non-point, bringing closure to your speaking segment. The next panelist begins and you're not sure what you just said.

In the scenario above, you are most likely unaware of the meandering journey you just took. It likely made sense in your mind, and your stream-of-consciousness speech had a beginning, a middle, and an end. However, your audience and fellow panelists are left asking, "What's your point?"

We do this all the time. It is easy to see when you're standing in front of a group. The bigger problem is the countless conversations happening more intimately. Pointless blathering that poses as meaningful conversation permeates our daily interactions. The smaller stakes reduce the downside impact of pointlessness, but the problems remain: missed opportunities to say something meaningful and/or the waste of someone's time and attention.

Communicator In Chief

The critical nature of communication becomes very apparent in our daily roles. During a recent interview, I was asked about my daily activities in my role as CEO of Northwind Pharmaceuticals. As I sifted through a typical day in my life, I realized that I spend most of my time communicating. There are some tasks on which I work, but the vast majority of my time is spent writing, emailing, talking, and listening— not necessarily in that order. It makes complete sense to me, but I had never really considered how much I live in the space of communication.

The next question she asked focused on the education necessary to be successful in my "career." Did the college courses I took relate to what I do today? Once again, I came back to communication. The classes I best remember are the ones in which I had to distill the essence of an idea and present it intelligibly, in written or verbal form. These were my most challenging and most satisfying courses. They required me to think, pull those thoughts together, and articulate them to another human being concisely. Some of that may simply be my preference, but I think it goes deeper.

Her final question was: what key skills would someone else need to be successful in what I'm doing? My answer didn't change much. After getting past a few platitudes on perseverance (which really boils down to a person's ability to take punches repeatedly), I came back to communication. To truly be effective in my role, I have to be concise and compelling in my outbound communication, and I have to get to the heart of inbound communication. Not one-way, sermonizing, always-talking communication. Real, give-and-take human interaction. Effective communication with other people is the most critical aspect of my job.

I'm frequently asked how I find time to write. For me, it is an extension of what I'm doing all day long. Typically, I'm just relaying my experiences with other people. It's what I do. However, writing about those experiences is just one element. The bigger part is being present in the many interactions of my day. Listening to reports, challenges, questions, concerns, ideas, hopes, dreams, and fears. As the CEO, my job is less about answering the queries and concerns and more about making myself available. Ultimately, communication *IS* my job, and the more interactive, the better.

Be a Great Communicator, Every Day

When you stand for something, you do have something important to say. Your beliefs, knowledge, and perspectives are unique in this world. Your experiences are unique. You bring that uniqueness to every interaction, and the world deserves to understand your point of view. You don't need to epitomize heavenly eloquence, but you owe it to the people around you to get better at making our point. You deserve, *and they deserve*, your best efforts to be better communicators.

A recent panel discussion gave me the opportunity to observe some interesting communication dynamics and identify some ways we can all improve in our conversations with those around us. From that experience, I distilled the following ten points on being a great communicator:

1. **Be Prepared**. Mark Twain once said, "It usually takes me more than three weeks to prepare a good impromptu speech." Obviously, we can't be prepared for every conversational situation, but we can be ready for meetings, calls, and topical discussions. A simple list of two to three key points and/or objectives can go a long way to making the conversation more meaningful.

2. **Be Concise**. The Churchill quotation at the beginning of this essay captures it nicely. What is the shortest path to making your point? An economy of words implies command of your subject matter and clarity of thinking. You can always add more words later on, but you can never take them away.

3. **Be Interesting**. Any point of view is made more powerful by being delivered in an interesting fashion. Some people are good storytellers. I personally find it easier to reference others who are far more brilliant than I. There are plenty of anecdotes, movies, songs, poems, articles, and other pieces of brilliance out there to support any point you want to make. Use them.

4. **Be Expressive**. This is the sister to #3 above. Intonation, facial expressions, and colorful language make you more engaging and interesting. Efforts to be expressive support your point by making you and your message real to your audience.

5. **Be Empathetic**. One of the biggest mistakes people make when talking to others is focusing on their own side of the conversation and losing track of what's happening on the other side. If you want to engage someone with your message, you need to be tuned in to what they are thinking, feeling, and conveying. So often we hear their words but don't listen. Understand that this is happening on the other end as well. When you demonstrate your empathy, it draws the other person in and they seek to understand. This also applies to recognizing when you lose people while you are talking. Read the signs.

6. **Be Patient**. We often tend to blather when speaking because we are afraid that we might not get to finish our thought or that we might forget our point. In this case, we "machine gun" every random thought directly at the audience and our message becomes frenetic. Patience gives us the opportunity for the discussion to unfold and allows us to remain calm enough to deliver our message at a measured, digestible pace. It also helps us remember our key points because we are more relaxed.

7. **Be Flexible**. The best communication evolves with the conversation. There are times to stay on point, and then there are moments

that something more compelling happens in a new conversational direction. You can often make your best point by allowing someone to take you in a direction that makes it more meaningful to them.

8. **Be Intentional**. Taking a free-ranging verbal journey is very easy for us. To focus our message and make our point, we must be intentional in returning to the original path and disciplining ourselves to repeat as necessary. Being intentional isn't inflexibility; it is understanding our objective and working our plan.

9. **Be Respectful**. See yourself as a steward of the other person's time. They are not there as a release valve for your prattle. When you respect another person's time, you naturally seek to minimize your impact on it and work to bring value for their investment. Are you giving them all that you can for their investment of time and attention?

10. **Be Inviting**. Finally, invite your audience to contribute. The best conversation is an exchange of meaningful ideas. Seeking the input of your audience brings them along with you, forces them to pay attention to your message, and helps you gauge their level of interest and engagement. Your odds of making an impact (and your point) will be much greater if you are able to pull your audience into the discussion.

Not every conversation needs to be profound, but they all should honor the time of those involved. Whether we're presenting to a room of people or talking one-on-one with a colleague, our days are full of opportunities to be better communicators. Like it or not, we are judged by our ability to articulate thoughts and ideas. Putting the effort into improving your communications skills will make you more effective, improve your interactions with other people, and deepen your thinking on the topics you find most interesting.

People, Assumptions, and the Stories We Tell Ourselves

But I'm quite sure that you'll tell me
Just how I should feel today.
—New Order, "Blue Monday"

Our ability to effectively make our point enables the world to know where we stand. However, there is an additional element in the communication equation, and it can be a barrier no matter how clear and concise our message. Let's consider the filters through which all messages must pass.

Have you ever considered the bookshelf full of stories you take with you into your place of work, your classroom, or your kitchen? All of us are incredibly imaginative when it comes to creating our own realities. Often, we are particularly adept at fabricating someone else's perceptions. In 1983, New Order released "Blue Monday," a song that has always made me consider the complexities that occur in communications between people: "I'm quite sure that you'll tell me just how I should feel today." We experience this in all of our relationships and interactions. We see, hear, or anticipate another person through our own filter and finish their story for them. If we are somewhat effective at guessing, we are said to be "emotionally intelligent." If we get the story wrong, we are insensitive, oblivious, ignorant, uncaring, or simply mistaken. Men, women, children, adults…it happens with all of us.

As managers and leaders, we set direction, define objectives, clarify vision, and hold people accountable. For us, it is always clear because we see it in our minds. When we speak or write, it is clear for us because we know what we mean. However, I continue to find that no matter how clear I feel that I'm being in my communication, my words still get translated through the filter of my audience and they make them their own. This generally isn't terribly problematic for things that are easily measured; clear metrics make communication easy and expectations quite clear. Translation issues occur when our filter takes the words we hear and overlays them with our self-image, doubts, fears, hopes, or expectations. When we "make them our own," those words morph into a different narrative—one that we've created. Quite often one that isn't real...until we make it real.

> We see, hear, or anticipate another person through our own filter and finish their story for them.

We are all aware of it, yet we continue to do it. Why? For one thing, we are blessed and cursed with the glories of higher intelligence. Reading a situation and anticipating possible outcomes is an incredibly complex capability and very necessary for our survival. The issue isn't our ability to anticipate, the issue is in the assumptions we make in how we anticipate. Felix from the *Odd Couple* famously described for us what happens when we make assumptions: "When you assume, you make an ass out of you and me." Our assumptions are based on how we see the world and ourselves. They are built upon the story we tell our selves about everything we experience. When New Order suggested that "You'll tell me just how I should feel," they were describing our tendency to project our story onto another person—a story built upon our assumptions.

With time, our assumptions and how we apply them can become even more challenging. Over time, we create a large, carefully curated collection of assumptions and narratives. Our story evolves, and we bring in new characters assigned to the roles necessary to fulfill that narrative. Yes, we build wisdom, and our anticipation skills evolve as well. Unfortunately, much of our progress gets lost in the narrative we've written. We build a collection of baggage that taints much of the communication we experience with other people. When we harbor self-doubt, negativity, or fear, we begin to write a self-fulfilling narrative in our relationships and our lives. We assume all sorts of things about other people's intentions, expectations, and sincerity. These assumptions frequently take us exactly where we imagined.

What's the answer? I'm afraid that a one-way psychoanalysis won't help much. You know and understand your filters much more than I ever will. After all, it is your narrative. However, I do believe we can cultivate some habits and attitudes for managing the challenges of our assumptions. If you need to assume, start with these:

1. **Assume the best intentions in other people**. Yes, I know this is risky. Yes, I know you've been burned. But I also know that until you can give someone else the benefit of the doubt, you will not be able to overcome the gap between you. Start with a belief in good intentions, and it might change the narrative. You can always change your mind later.

2. **Assume they mean what they say**. Often, we look for hidden meanings. We like to "read between the lines." This is such a source of problems in our communications with others. Sometimes, we need to just take what someone says at face value. After all, you can't control their intentions, but you can control what you do and say.

3. **Assume there is common ground**. When our narrative puts us at odds with another person, it inhibits our ability to build a constructive relationship. When we can find a point of intersection for our interests, that common ground can create a lot of positive energy and change the story we are telling ourselves (and the story they are telling themselves).

4. **Assume that you are good, capable, and important**. Now we get to the crux of the matter. The biggest barrier in our narrative is our own self-image. It manifests itself in everything we do, say, or imagine. Self-doubt appears in how we look at other people and how we hear their words or read their behavior. If you want to maximize your interactions with others, you've got to be honest with yourself about your self-image. We wrap our sense of worth up with everything around us—once you acknowledge this, you can move on to giving yourself the benefit of the doubt. Change how you talk to yourself. Change the story you tell yourself. Write a happy ending and walk toward it.

5. **Assume that you will survive when they let you down**. Have you been telling yourself another story as you read this essay? The self-protective story reminding you that there is no way you are going to make assumptions that will give another person the chance to hurt, disappoint, or fail you? My final suggestion is that you take the risk anyway and convince yourself that you will survive. You're going to be let down. You will overcome it.

Now you are free. You are free to take your story in your best direction. You are free to leverage all of your gifts and talents to do your best. You are free to fail and pick yourself back up again. Yeah, there is going to be some disappointment. So what? Quit worrying about it and get on with living a full life. When we write our narrative with expansive thinking, positive energy, hope in possibility, belief in our self, and belief in other people, anything is possible.

Effective Dissent and the Dangers of Contempt

Contempt is the weapon of the weak and a defense against one's own despised and unwanted feelings.
—*Alice Miller*

A very real downside to standing for something every day is the fact that there will be people who do not agree with you. Disagreement in and of itself is not a bad thing. In fact, disagreement can be an effective way to solve problems, discover new solutions, and expand horizons. The challenge is finding a way to constructively disagree.

In 1998's *Saving Private Ryan*, Captain Miller (played by Tom Hanks) coaches his squad on the proper way to complain:

Private Jackson: Sir...I have an opinion on this matter.

Captain Miller: Well, by all means, share it with the squad.

Private Jackson: Well, from my way of thinking, sir, this entire mission is a serious misallocation of valuable military resources.

Captain Miller: Yeah. Go on.

Private Jackson: Well, it seems to me, sir, that God gave me a special gift, made me a fine instrument of warfare.

Captain Miller: Reiben, pay attention. Now, this is the way to gripe. Continue, Jackson.

Private Jackson: Well, what I mean by that, sir, is…if you was to put me and this here sniper rifle anywhere up to and including one mile of Adolf Hitler with a clear line of sight, sir…pack your bags, fellas, war's over. Amen.

From there, Miller goes on to clarify the chain of command as it relates to griping: "I don't gripe to you, Reiben. I'm a captain. There's a chain of command. Gripes go up, not down. Always up. You gripe to me, I gripe to my superior officer, so on, so on, and so on. I don't gripe to you. I don't gripe in front of you."

Finally, Captain Miller completes the lesson with an example of how he would communicate dissent with his commanding office:

Private Reiben: I'm sorry, sir, but uh…let's say you weren't a captain, or maybe I was a major. What would you say then?

Captain Miller: Well, in that case…I'd say, "This is an excellent mission, sir, with an extremely valuable objective, sir, worthy of my best efforts, sir. Moreover…I feel heartfelt sorrow for the mother of Private James Ryan and am willing to lay down my life and the lives of my men—especially you, Reiben—to ease her suffering."

Miller's tongue-in-cheek response reinforces his message and shows his team the way. It is one of many great scenes in the movie and provides a powerful demonstration of leadership, the effective use of the complaint, and the art of "managing up."

There will always be disagreement. It is simply the nature of being a human among other humans. To expect otherwise is unrealistic and will lead to certain frustration. For the savvy professional, there is opportunity here. Why? Because we have become ineffective at disagreeing. Dissent has turned into whining, and rather than logically articulating counterpoints, many choose to "go nuclear" by attacking with the biggest weapon they have. Unfortunately, this usually involves an expletive or name-calling.

Why not? We watch political debates devolve into name-calling. Our press focuses on the negative energy in soundbites and stories. We laugh at YouTube videos that show someone going "ballistic" on another person and "winning" through tirade.

The problem with these lapses in civility is that they not only undermine the situation and the process of finding a better solution, they undermine the person. Underlying aggressive argumentation is an inability to cope. We can't handle people who disagree with us. We don't want to try. It is easier to dislike them. It is easier to tear them down. It is easier to call them names.

It is one thing to disagree with a stranger on the street and then walk away, never to see them again. We do this all the time in our cars—the ultimate platform for the caveman response to indignity. But what happens in the workplace? What happens in our relationships? Without the ability to constructively disagree with another person, we cannot resolve our differences. We fume. We pout. We plot. Perhaps we were wrong and won't admit it. Perhaps our opponent is more articulate or faster on her feet. Perhaps we are so clearly "right" that it is below us to even argue our point. Maybe it's just safer to say nothing.

Our Dangerous World of Contempt

In his book *Blink*, Malcolm Gladwell introduces his premise with the story of a study conducted over many years focusing on the nature of relationships. A researcher would bring couples into the lab, ask them to discuss a topic on which they disagreed, and then proceed to record and observe the entire interaction. Over the years, the researcher became very adept at predicting whether a relationship would last, based on his observations during these brief encounters. One of the key variables in the researcher's analysis revolved around the notion of contempt. In the situations in which contempt was observed in the tone or reaction by one or both parties, it was almost always an indicator of an eventual failure in the relationship.

Since reading that portion of Gladwell's book, I've looked at the word "contempt" differently. We've often heard the term used relative to our legal system; one is sometimes held in "contempt of court." As it relates to our legal system, contempt is the offence of being disobedient or disrespectful toward a court of law and its officers in the form of behavior that opposes or defies the authority, justice, and dignity of the court. Our legal definition doesn't quite capture the gravity of the word as it relates to our interactions with other people.

Contempt is defined as "the feeling that a person or a thing is beneath consideration, worthless, or deserving scorn." In the research referenced above, it was the death knell for intimate relationships between couples. If the state of contempt is so destructive to close, personal relationships, imagine what it does to less intimate relationships that weave throughout our society.

During the election season of 2016, I was reminded of the word contempt as I saw a news article talking about a billionaire's donation to one of the presidential campaigns. The article included several Twitter feeds posted by high-profile people reacting to the news of the donation. I was astonished to read how vicious the tweets were. The headline of one tweet said: "F*** You _____!" This wasn't a bunch of teenagers bullying their classmates. These were tweets coming from adult leaders in various high-level positions with corporations and other organizations within our country. Put aside for a moment the lack of professionalism in blasting that sort of rhetoric into the media sphere and consider the scope of the emotion behind that tweet. That is CONTEMPT with a capital 'C'!

I realize that I should not be surprised—our world has become quite comfortable with outbursts, tantrums, and ill-considered social media assaults of all flavors. The aforementioned election upped the ante on these outbursts, with more and more individuals and organizations trying to push the bar lower and lower in the landscape of uncivil discourse. However, I WAS surprised, and saddened, by what I read. In reading the article and the tweets, there was no argument explaining why the donation was a bad idea. There was no counterpoint to the logic behind such a donation or even an attempt to understand why the billionaire would make the donation. Every bit of what I read was steeped in contempt for another thinking, breathing, and feeling human being. Those tweeting weren't attacking his ideas, they were attacking him as a person.

Argument and disagreement have been happening for centuries. The American political tradition has always been one of bare-fisted disagreement, and the 2016 election cycle was no different. The problem is that we are no longer arguing over ideas and philosophies. We are substituting anger and emotion for reason and logic while undermining our own points and the system we've built to compromise on differences. Complex problems get reduced to sound-bite rallying cries branded under clever names like "black lives matter," "white privilege," "social justice," "gun control," "pro-life," or even "Democrat" and "Republican." These are big, broad buckets that come to represent absolute positions for or against rather than the highly nuanced realities of millions of people trying to live together under one flag. We line up on either side of the line and assume the worst about everyone with the opposing view. The biggest danger of our simmering contempt is that it leaves no room for reconciliation when the dust has settled. Contempt forms the basis for ongoing dislike, disagreement, and distrust, while sowing the seeds for the escalation of our arguments in increasingly less civil ways.

Our current political environment reflects an unapologetic embrace of contempt. The scorn heaped upon Donald Trump as president may be unparalleled in the history of our country. For his part, Trump almost seems to relish it. The brawling, no-holds-barred, nature of our political environment mirrors what is happening on our streets. Protesters gather looking for a fight and often seem unaware of why they are even protesting. We aren't protesting for change, ideas, or rational argument, we are simply ranting as we work to bury our opponents in noise, vitriol, and sometimes violence. Politicians, talk show hosts, and the news media work to stir it up…and why? Because it generates attention, viewership, and revenue.

While we are locked in our political race to the bottom, we see the signs of contempt seeping into our business and personal dealings. Social media puts this on full display. Aggressive tweets are one form, but it happens on multiple fronts. Attacks on people associated with certain companies. Dark criticism of shares and posts regardless of reason or intent. Mean-spirited confrontations in the office or on the street should anyone choose to disagree with another's point of view. Our contempt is spilling over far beyond the political arena.

In addition to the obvious external implications of contempt for our relationships and other people, there is a deeper danger to us as human beings. Contempt is a dark, very negative feeling. It is a cousin to hatred and far more insidious. It is often subtle and hides itself behind smart words and self-righteousness. Harboring contempt lessens us. It brings us lower with a slow-drip negativity that undermines hope and optimism. Contempt breeds cynicism and blocks the creative energies that enable us to be all of which we are capable. It doesn't just hurt those around us.

Constructive Dissent

As leaders, one of the greatest gifts we can give our team is a safe environment to disagree. We are taught that dissent brings new ideas, fresh perspectives, and helps us step outside of potentially narrow thinking. Are you seeing this in your work environment? Do you have people step up in a meeting and tell you that your idea will not work? Why is dissent such a dangerous thing? Because we don't do it well.

Many people would say that it is simply common sense to think before you speak or consider the audience when making a point. But so often, emotion gets the better of us, and we assault rather than constructively disagree. My belief is that many people don't know how to engage in constructive dissent. This is not only an unfortunate situation for the individual, it is devastating for the organization. If your team cannot provide constructive disagreement, it not only hurts relationships and morale, the organization loses a powerful catalyst for change and improvement. Great ideas are lost in moments that devolve into emotional assaults because we become too concerned about winning and lose sight of the opportunities in disagreement.

The issue, and opportunity, goes far beyond our organizations. Small interactions on social media, in the coffee shop, at school, or in the kitchen present the opportunity for disagreement as well as also the opportunity to rise above it. Dissent doesn't have to devolve into violent protest or relationship destroying ill-will. We don't have to view anyone who disagrees with us as the enemy. We must resist this inclination and seek paths to constructive disagreement.

Whether you are formally a leader in your organization or a contributing team member, your best interests are served when you, your peers, and your team disagree in a civil and constructive fashion. The same can be said for our daily encounters. Here are a few points to consider when facing a confrontation:

- **Put yourself in the other person's shoes.**

- **When you feel emotional, step back** and ask yourself: "What do I gain by sharing what I'm thinking in this moment?"

- **Consider why you disagree.** Is it selfish motivation or do you have a legitimate concern? Understand your own motives. Sincerity trumps emotion.

- **What is your objective?** What is the ideal result? Channel your inner chess player and think a few moves ahead. Is your current path taking you there?

- **Read your audience.** Again, read your audience. Have you lost them? Are they digging in? If so, then pull back and take another tack. Seek first to understand, then to be understood.

- **Where is the win for all concerned?** Look for a mutual win and you'll feel the tone of the conversation shift.

- **Assume good intent.** If you can't assume good intent on the part of the other person, you need to consider your own motivations and if you are in the right place. If you can find the good intent, then you might find a point on the path where you can meet.

- **Seek knowledge first.** Be well-read. Be well-informed. Then use that knowledge constructively.

- **Open your heart.** An open heart is a difficult place to harbor contempt.

- **Understand why you believe as you do.** If you can't understand your position, why should someone else? If it is hard for you to articulate, write it down first, then read it aloud.

- **Resist your biases.** Prejudice of one flavor or another (there are many types besides racial) always influences our positions. Recognize it and rise above it.

An inability to cope with disagreement is at the root of our loss of civility and a huge barrier in our ability to effectively stand for something.

It is easier to simply dislike someone than to argue with them. The generous nature of this premise assumes that both parties are well-informed but simply choose to not put the effort into debating their positions. A darker issue fueling deeper contempt lies in the fact that we are frequently uninformed or uneducated about a particular issue, so aggressive attacks become the substitute for rational argumentation. This is easily seen in fabricated videos, emails, and other detritus scattered among our social media pages and inboxes. Our contempt makes it easy to rationalize uninformed attacks and deliberately avoid educating ourselves more fully on the issues.

Now is the time for strong, principled leadership—and not just from our "leaders." The good news is that we can all lead the way. In our churches, on our Facebook pages, in our offices, on our phones, in front of employees, and behind their backs…we can choose to set the example of sincere, informed discourse. We can say no to personal attacks and ask why someone feels as they do. We can encourage educated debate and set the tone in how we communicate and, more importantly, how we disagree. Whether you are a CEO, a clerk, a nurse, or a politician, you can make your own difference and show those in your world that you won't give in to the contempt.

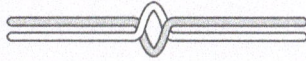

You Can't Manage Your Critics

You have enemies? Good. That means you've stood up for something,
sometime in your life.
—Winston S. Churchill

Now that you've put yourself out there and made it clear where you stand, you will attract critics. There is a place to have rational dissent, and then there is the world of your critics. There is a time to engage in the argument, and there is a time to understand that some hearts will not be changed.

I find it quite astounding how far people will go to tear down other human beings. It seems that no matter the accomplishment, intent, or even the reality, there will be one or more individuals perfectly willing to find the fault, failing, or downside. In many ways, criticism can result in something good: finding weaknesses in an argument, offering a different perspective, pushing someone to be better, or revealing truly reprehensible behavior on the part of other people. These results might be defined as constructive.

The sad truth is that much of it is not constructive. Often, criticism is more about the one offering it than its intended target. Anyone is fair game. Politicians, entrepreneurs, civic leaders, philanthropists, relatives...anyone. Somehow, someway, we feel that tearing someone else down will make us more. Of course, we don't admit that. No one wants to admit that their feelings of inadequacy or jealousy prompt them to attack someone else. Few will acknowledge that their efforts to criticize another person or organization are actually about trying to further their own cause or improve their position. Competitive or not, it really doesn't matter. We're seemingly hard-wired to enjoy, or at least be entertained by, watching someone fall, and the critics know it.

Knowing this, why do we put so much effort into the argument? There are times when criticism must be addressed. Often, it is simply damage control. Facebook's efforts to manage the firestorm around the privacy of its users is exactly that: damage control. Of course, the criticism of the company, and the industry, won't stop because of their follow-up actions. There are too many competing interests. In this case, they hope to manage the narrative, knowing they have no hope in managing the critics.

For most of us, arguing with critics is our way of affirming our "rightness." Surely that person doesn't understand my point, or they wouldn't be disagreeing, right? Perhaps in a one-on-one conversation, you might convert someone. Perhaps. The reality is that your point likely has nothing to do with their criticism. Not if they feel somehow empowered or better about themselves by attacking you or your point. Not if they feel that they might somehow improve their position if yours lessens. In most cases, trying to manage your critic is an exercise in futility.

A recent online CNN article had a headline that reads: "'Troubled individual:' Mother Teresa no saint to her critics." The article goes on to provide perspectives from two individuals. The first person describes poor conditions in the care facilities managed by the Missionaries of Charity. The other argues that the canonization of Mother Teresa is bogus because there is no such thing as miracles. In sixty-nine years of service and humility, Mother Teresa touched millions of lives, and still the criticism goes on. It seems that whatever you do, it will never be enough to please everyone.

It is easy to see the nature of criticism as it relates to the famous. To be famous is to be a magnet for criticism. What about the rest of us? We also endure it at every turn. People honk their criticism in traffic. People attack what you write. People tear you down behind your back. People criticize your faith, your clothes, your hair, your make-up, your selfishness, your generosity, your work, your effort, your thinking, your intentions. The truth of the matter is that anytime you put yourself out there in any way (even if you don't intend to), you are inviting a critic into your life. It is inescapable.

As much as we know and understand the nature of the critic, it still hurts. Famous writers and entertainers talk about their battles with critics and haters and the ensuing doubt. Chefs, artists, singers…everyone who has put themselves out there has battled with their critics. Executives, doctors, moms, and saints…no one is immune. Those successful in living with it also all pretty much give the same counsel: ignore it. You can argue with it, but it won't change anything. You can't change it. Your work won't appeal to everyone. You can't manage your critics.

However, you can manage yourself. You can surround yourself with believers. You can focus on your own best intentions and those things that are within your control. You can improve your work and evolve your perspective. You can trust yourself and those you love. After all, why do they love you? You can put yourself in situations to succeed, and you can choose how you react to your failures. Ultimately, critics are about what you can't control. You win by focusing on what you can control.

So, the next time you read that article or tweet attacking your favorite saint, your favorite singer, your next-door neighbor, or something else in which you believe, take a breath and pause. Consider the perspective of the criticizer and focus on why you feel differently. Perhaps by engaging a bit more empathy we might move the critical needle of negativity toward the positive. Maybe focusing on the worth of a person's work or the impact of someone's efforts will remind us that we are worthy and that our work is also making a difference. Remember that you can't manage your critics, but you can choose self-compassion and to continue to do your best work in the pursuit of standing for something in which you believe.

Aiming for the Stars

Critics have said Mr. Musk's goals are overly ambitious…
—Andy Pasztor, The Wall Street Journal

When Elon Musk publicly announced plans to build the most powerful rocket ever and use it to launch a manned mission to Mars by 2024, the announcement was described as his "most aggressive expression yet of his vision for privately funded space exploration." Aggressive? Perhaps. Bold. Absolutely. Who else names their rocket BFR? I love it.

Though I don't share Musk's passion to get people to Mars, I am cheering him on. One of the deliciously compelling elements of Musk's vision is the reaction it elicits from all the naysayers. They say it's too expensive, that SpaceX (Musk's rocket producing company) can't generate the free cash flows to cover the estimated $10 billion mission cost. They point to other goals and deadlines that Musk has missed over the years, saying that he's underestimating the difficulty. They say, they say, they say. I say: go for it.

Guess what? This is a man who built a multi-billion-dollar company *because* of his vision to get people to Mars. SpaceX overcame amazing odds to get its first rocket launched in 2008 and evolve into a powerhouse space company that has gone from startup to six thousand employees in fifteen years. Curious about just how unlikely that evolution has been? Read Ashlee Vance's

> Freedom lies in being bold.
> —Robert Frost

biography, *Elon Musk: Tesla, SpaceX, and the Quest for a Fantastic Future.* Musk's journey has been amazing not just for the scale of his success but even more so for the scope of what he has had to overcome. His gifts as a problem-solver are unparalleled.

Success always invites criticism, and Musk's story is no different. However, the most inspiring aspect of Elon Musk's entrepreneurial journey may be his willingness to confess big, bold dreams and then relentlessly pursue them. The admission that SpaceX's true objective is a mission to Mars is the latest in a long series of what I view as "Babe Ruth" moments, a reference to Ruth's legend of pointing to the stands to indicate where he planned to put his next home run. Musk has been unflinching in his willingness to share bold plans and take the ridicule that such dreaming incurs...all while making them happen. His bold steps have been shadowed by the persistent and often craven criticism of those with lesser dreams and ample negativity, criticism potentially born from the dark corners of envy.

What happens when we aim for the stars? What seed is sown when we first ask the question why not? Recent generations have been criticized for not dreaming big enough, for not seeking outlandish, world-changing visions. We've traded complex, multi-year planning focused on big dreams for the short-term view of quarterly results and two- or four-year election cycles. We've exchanged cheering the bold dreamers and their plans for a bigger future with jeering at failed attempts at boldness. There are still big dreamers in our midst, but the safer road is the quiet pursuit of those visions lest we bring energy draining ridicule and criticism.

The first step in achieving something bold is imagining that you might. Each of us has an element of boldness, and not all dreams have to be for other planets. However, in aiming at the stars, even a miss might take us somewhere new and exciting. The next time you see a piece criticizing someone's bold vision or crazy dream, look beyond the headline or soundbite. Ask yourself, what if? What if he or she achieved that crazy dream? There are always plenty of reasons why things might not work. *Maybe it's time we started finding the reasons for why it makes sense to pursue them anyway.*

Choose Happiness Every Day

Time is precious. So often, we allow the world to determine our state of mind for the time we have been given. Decide right now on what your mind will dwell. Choose happiness every day.

Is Happiness a Choice?

Folks are usually about as happy as they make their minds up to be.
—Abraham Lincoln

Happiness appears to be on the minds of many these days as we see scores of books and other media appearing to tell us more about it and help us get there. I suppose it makes sense to talk about happiness in a world that seems so full of unhappiness. People everywhere are struggling with depression, addiction, and pain of all varieties. Perhaps the notion of happiness is more relevant than ever. Even our country was founded on the idea that the "pursuit of happiness" is an inalienable right. It seems that the topic has been on our collective mind for a very long time.

What Is Happiness?

The concept of happiness appeared on my radar during a recent conversation with business owners about growth. In that discussion, I was pressing the group on being intentional with their planning around growth. The conversation started with the question: "Where do you see your business in three to five years?" One of the entrepreneurs responded with the story of a market owner who had been very successful in building a business but hated working in it; his point was that he wanted to align his growth with being happy. As I considered his response, I felt hesitant: on the one hand it made perfect sense, but on another level, something seemed problematic with using happiness as a reference point for setting strategy as an objective in and of itself.

Merriam-Webster defines happiness as "a state of well-being and contentment." The entrepreneur's response makes perfect sense; who wouldn't want to align the growth of their business or their life with well-being and contentment? The fundamental problem with using happiness as a reference point is that it reflects a feeling, and feelings change. In fact, our feelings are a tremendous source of issues around confidence, fear, inspiration, determination, motivation, doubt, and on and on. Trusting our feelings is tricky business when it comes to mapping a life well-lived. How many of us would have finished high school if we had been allowed to follow our feelings? How many other things would be left unfinished if we hadn't pushed through some point of unhappiness?

What Makes *You* Happy?

The issue with happiness as a reference point does not stop with its shaky pillars of feelings. We often talk about doing things that "make us happy." We want to be around people who "make us happy." We talk about happiness in holistic terms as if it is an end-state, and anything that does not lead us to this end-state is wrong or unhealthy. Expecting someone or something else to "make us happy" is a sure path to disappointment. Not because they failed us, but because we failed to realize that no one exists to make another person happy. In a similar fashion, our pursuits do not exist to make us happy—though we may feel happiness while pursuing them.

Wait, our pursuits don't exist to make us happy? Why would I pursue something that doesn't make me happy? My father-in-law used to describe happiness as a byproduct, not part of the equation. There is no road map or path that leads directly to happiness. We find ourselves there by living fully, by pursuing the best version of our self. Happiness should not be an objective for its own sake, it comes from our efforts to live our best life. It comes from using our gifts to their fullest while becoming the best people we can be. Our pursuits don't exist to make us happy, but we may feel happiness while pursuing them.

The Paradox of Happiness

Another issue with happiness as an endpoint is that, by its nature, it is a selfish pursuit. Herein lies the paradox. As we pursue happiness, we are in fact chasing our own gratification, and the more we gratify ourselves the shorter lived is our state of being happy. How does this occur? Because happiness ultimately stems from what we give. If our greatest gifts are the ones that multiply when given away, what does that say about what we keep to ourselves? The irony is that we find happiness when we don't pursue it and focus instead on giving the best of ourselves. In the end, we are the greatest determiners of our own happiness.

Let's summarize some basic tenets of happiness:

1. Happiness comes from within.

2. YOU are the determining factor of your happiness. Your attitude is the driver.

3. Being all that you can be drives happiness.

4. Giving selflessly feeds happiness.

Happiness is not:

- a feel-good life

- an easy life

- getting everything you want

- winning all the time

- avoiding disappointment

Happiness will result from:

- overcoming adversity

- recovering from hurt

- having a worthy objective

- seeing possibility and seeking it

- embracing hope

- believing in yourself

- believing in others

- giving of yourself fully

- loving fully

- forgiving

- doing the right thing

- seeking excellence

- allowing others to love you

A Happy By-Product

When I consider my conversation with that group of entrepreneurs, it is clear to me that making happiness the objective when setting the direction of your business, or your life, is not a good idea. Happiness is not an endpoint, it is a by-product. That doesn't mean that you shouldn't balance priorities and preferences when pursuing work, family, hobby, social, or any other investments of your time. Investing yourself fully in your priorities may result in the by-product of happiness, but you can't get there directly.

One final note. Like feelings, your priorities will change with different phases of your life. That is perfectly fine. Remember that the principles that lead to a life well-lived (and therein happiness) will not change. A life well-lived demands that we give our best, love our best, and forgive as best we can. The better we can live these foundational principles, the closer we will live to happiness. You might find that the wonderful by-product of living this way is that you no longer worry about being happy.

Choose Joy Every Day

Joy is what happens to us when we allow ourselves to recognize how good things really are.
—Marianne Williamson

The crowd was electric with anticipation. The lights were low. The background music was barely audible as eighteen thousand individuals contributed their own buzz to the arena. In seconds, the band would burst on the scene, releasing these minutes of tension with their unique blend of music, song, and energy. There was power in this moment. An edge for which we were all hungry. Though none of us were performing, we were all part of the performance. We were raving fans, and we were ready to be taken somewhere else.

The place was Indianapolis. The band was Coldplay. The experience was amazing. Everything about the show was world-class. The stage, the lights, and the entire production were a feast for the eyes and the ears. The band itself has achieved epic success commercially and, after seven albums, is at the top of its game. Their latest production, "Head Full of Dreams," is a tour de force of color, movement, and sound worthy of our biggest stages.

Though I enjoy their music, something else struck me as I watched my first live Coldplay performance. Yes, the pageantry was entertaining, and I knew the words to many of the songs, but there was something else happening on the stage and in the production. I felt something.

Their front man, Chris Martin, was incredibly energetic as he moved up and down the stage and engaged the crowd. Clearly very talented as a singer and musician, he matched, perhaps exceeded, those talents as a performer. The crowd roared. I looked around to see everyone around me singing, dancing, and smiling. And there it was: joy.

During the concert, there were balloons, beach balls, and thousands of flashing wristbands carefully orchestrated to the performance. A curious piece of branding was a little plastic pin given to attendees that said "Love." A grand marketing scheme executed to the tiniest detail. I wondered, "What are they selling?"

Looking back to the stage, I saw it again: joy. It was an image and sensation I couldn't shake. The crowd was having fun…but so was the band. It wasn't just fun in an "I'm feeling entertained" kind of way. It was joy. Real, my-face-hurts-from-smiling kind of joy. The word "ebullient" came to mind as I watched Martin perform. The colors, words like "love," the name of the tour, the lights, and all of the production were well-branded, well-themed, and well-executed. However, the joy came from somewhere else.

I've written before on the nature of epic entertainment events and the power of emotion to draw us together. It is fun to be caught up in such expansive experiences, but I don't recall one in which I've witnessed such a sense of joy on the stage and in the crowd. Watching Martin and Coldplay on stage, I believe that the "love" symbol was not only strong branding, I believe it was sincere branding. In a very powerful way, they were able to convey it through the joy they exuded during their performance.

Clearly, we can't maintain epic levels of joy in every moment of every day. But there is a subtler joy that we can muster through our working lives. Part attitude, part conviction, and part vocation, we are called to find the joy in the mundane as well as the epic. Yes, called. In what we do and how we choose to do it. We have such capacity for joy and continue to deny ourselves through our choices, active and reactive.

It is so easy to fall into the habit of depletion: the state of allowing our day's energy vampires to drain us. Giving in to the negative distractions that keep us from the fulfillment of true joy, we muddle through. It seems like such a waste. Why can't we find even a small piece of that Coldplay-level joy in our working day?

Start by reminding yourself that it doesn't have to be epic to be special. It doesn't have to be a complex production, and you don't have to wait for it. The great thing about joy is that it is a choice. Another pop star, Madonna, said, "Poor is the man whose pleasure depends on the permission of another." I'd like to modify that line and suggest that we are all poor who wait for others to bring us joy. Don't wait.

Phillip Berry

You Deserve Sunny's Enthusiasm

Inside I am really bursting with boyish merriment; but I acted the paralytic Professor so well, that now I can't leave off.
—G.K. Chesterton, *The Man Who Was Thursday: A Nightmare*

We have a Cavalier King Charles Spaniel named Sunny. She is twelve years old. Normally, she spends her days sleeping, and when she decides to move, she typically moves slowly. The word "saunter" seems to catch the general essence of her movements. At this stage of her life, Sunny is friendly and loving but exhibits little energy for most distractions. This all changes twice a day.

For Sunny, the very notion of food being moved toward her bowl sends her into a fit of enthusiasm. This slow-moving dog (webmd.com says Sunny is the equivalent of about sixty-nine in human years) comes to life twice a day when she is fed. I'm not talking about a slight skip in her step; at the thought of food, Sunny explodes into a doggy dance that makes her look like a caramel and white colored bucking bronco gyrating across our kitchen floor. Her claws tap Astaire-like on the tile as she prances to her bowl. This joy of her life equates to an enthusiasm that turns her clock backward and makes her a puppy again.

As I watch Sunny, it makes me think of how I spend my days. When do I feel that kind of excitement? I recall thoughts of the Christmas season as a young boy; memories of unwrapping iconic gifts that still send shivers down my spine as I remember the thrill of moments past.

Excitement that made it difficult to sleep. Adulthood seems so effective at neutralizing that part of us which is capable of such childlike enthusiasm.

However, Sunny reminds us that those fires still burn, even if quietly. They lie deep within, waiting to be stoked, fueled with something that moves us. What moves you to such enthusiasm? Viewing every day as game day gives us the opportunity to embrace the adrenaline of competition, performance, or execution at our highest level. Enthusiasm comes from the same source. It is the thrill for something. The anticipation. The joy. It is there, and it is a fountain of youth.

A fountain of youth? Certainly. Enthusiasm puts a spring in our step. It takes away the aches and the pains as we focus our energies on something outside of our selves. Our energy surges as we engage in a more elemental way: heightened, on full alert, primal. Enthusiasm brings positive energy and empowers us to move quickly, think sharply, and focus all our senses in one direction—simultaneously, blissfully. Just look at Sunny: she becomes a peppy little puppy if I even hint at moving toward the bag of dog food. Pure joy.

Yes, there are differences between us as humans and my dog. Sunny is not burdened with all of the baggage we have to carry. Her aches and pains are simply a fact of life, she doesn't ask why or lament the difficulties. Simplicity can be such a blessing. However, her enthusiasm is a great model for all of us because it is so very simple. She has no control over it: the food-brain connection is an unconscious trigger for her, and exuberance ensues. Our gift is that we can trigger ourselves. We have the power to ignite our own enthusiasm.

We are blessed with big, powerful brains that respond to the levers we pull. If you want enthusiasm, simply pull the right lever. If you want joy, push the "joy" button. The levers and buttons are triggered by what we choose to think about, and how we choose to think about it. Our thoughts are so incredibly powerful. Sitting here right now,

I can conjure an image of a Christmas morning and feel excitement welling within. That is truly powerful. There is a smile on my face and my fingers feel twitchy with energy. Now, imagine all the thoughts of which you are capable.

As you begin to consider what you will do in the coming months, put those thoughts on your enthusiasm scale. Are you aspiring to things that move you in a deeply powerful way? Are you aiming too low or in the wrong direction? Do you feel your enthusiasm surge as you consider the first steps toward next year's objectives or the dreams lying beyond? Now, think of Sunny—if dogs are capable of smiling, I'm pretty sure that is a grin on her little doggy face as I scoop food into her bowl. You deserve nothing less.

NOTE: Our precious Sunny passed away in the Spring of 2018. Her joy and affection are sorely missed, but her example lives on.

In the Absence of Gratitude, We Find Entitlement

Death reminds us that life is a temporary privilege, not an endless right.
—Craig D. Lounsbrough

Every day, we wake up to a set of expectations. We expect that the sun will come up. We expect that the lights will come on when we flip the switch. We expect that our car will start. We expect the Keurig in our office to produce a tasty cup of coffee. So on and so forth. If any of these things don't happen, we feel disappointment. Why? Because we've come to expect them—we feel that we are entitled to them.

The dictionary defines "entitled" as "believing oneself to be inherently deserving of privileges or special treatment." The word "deserve" jumps out of this definition. Dangerous possibilities appear whenever we adopt a "deserve" disposition. When we feel we deserve something, we set ourselves up for an all-or-nothing confrontation with reality. If we get what we deserve, then all is right with the world. If we don't get what we deserve, we have been slighted. These powerful expectations can fuel disappointments on a massive scale. People can get aggressive when they don't receive what they are "owed."

Did you notice how the paragraph above moved from "entitled" to "owed"? The word "entitled" has a negative connotation. A person who feels "entitled" is often judged as unreasonable and undeserving.

However, receiving what you are "owed" is completely reasonable. This is the tricky nature of "entitlement" because we rationalize it to legitimacy by converting it to what we are "owed." If someone owes you something, you should collect, right?

The problem with a sense of entitlement is that it is the manifestation of the feeling that we are owed something, when in actuality that "something" is a privilege. We apply it to large and small things alike and when we don't get what we're owed, we become frustrated and negative; then we behave accordingly.

At its core, a sense of entitlement is the absence of gratitude. In gratitude, we adopt the attitude of one who is receiving a gift rather than what is owed. When we are grateful, we acknowledge a kindness, a moment, or an experience as something special. Something that perhaps we did not earn. Something that we may not deserve. Something that we are NOT owed.

Of course, there are transactions and interactions in which we are "owed" something. Our society is transactional, and it is normal in the course of our days. It is unacceptable for someone not to pay us for a service rendered. Revisit for a moment the definition of entitlement and consider the words "privileges or special treatment." What we are owed and what we feel we are entitled to can be very different things, and yet they are often confused.

When you start to look around the world, you realize that we've come to expect many things that might be considered amazing privileges to people from other nations. Lights that come on every time a switch is flipped? Wow! Clean water at the twist of a handle? Unbelievable! Anytime availability of an Internet connection with a steady stream of entertainment? Astounding!

Walk out into your world today and think about all of the little entitlements you have adopted in your day-to-day routine. Then step back from them and consider for a moment how they look through the lens of gratitude. The air in your lungs. The sun on your face. The kiss from a loved one. The dinner sitting on your table. The smile from a coworker. The opportunity to choose your path and walk it every day. The freedom to be yourself and live your life how you choose. Then consider how grateful you are for the tiniest of gifts you experience.

I suspect you may discover that the world really owes you very little and that the gifts you receive in a normal day are quite numerous. Appreciate them. Every...single...day.

Phillip Berry

Our Need for Control Leads to Disappointment

Freedom is the only worthy goal in life. It is won by disregarding things that lie beyond our control.
—Epictetus

More and more, I hear people talk about control. Control of their kids. Control of their jobs. Control of their relationships. Control. Just yesterday, I was told of someone who will not travel by airplane because of the anxiety caused by not being in control. Let's face it, a driving need for control over our world leads to numerous disappointments and coping issues.

At its heart, control is about getting what we want. It might be a thing or an outcome. The first point of disappointment occurs from a relative mentality—someone else is getting something we want (or deserve.) The root of much frustration lies in this scarcity mentality, the fear that a limited amount of something means we get less. The corollary is that we concern ourselves with fairness and become embittered when we perceive that someone does less than us but receives the same (or more). We attach our state of mind to a relative yardstick that measures our life against someone else. Our need for control has brought disappointment.

At work, we worry that others get better assignments, make more money, work less, or receive some other benefit that we don't. At home,

Choose Happiness Every Day ✳ 89

we concern ourselves with who does more chores, gives more in the relationship, or spends more of our collective money. On the road, we rage against the "takers" cutting in front of us in traffic or skirting traffic laws to their advantage. In society, we fume at special interest groups receiving a disproportionate share of government largess while we continue to pay our taxes and feel that we receive very little.

In these cases, our disappointments stem from how we view our position or situation relative to someone else. We want a certain outcome and we don't get it. Our fairness meter indicates that we have entered the red zone and we get irritated, lessening our joy due to factors that typically have little or nothing to do with us or our situation.

To be human is to be a bit obsessed with our relative situation. However, it is a recipe for disappointment. Why? Because we typically focus on things that are outside of our control. Stephen Covey described this in terms of a Circle of Influence and a Circle of Concern. Concern is the broad landscape of the world around us, over which we have absolutely no control or influence. Influence is the smaller bit of the world that is more immediate and accessible. Spending time in the Circle of Concern is counterproductive and often quite frustrating.

Recognizing that you are allowing the outside world to pollute your frame of mind is one thing. Taking action to control your attitude and focus on those things that you can influence is entirely different. It is much easier said than done and requires tremendous intention and discipline. Even then, you will fail from time to time. Here are some things to tell and ask yourself when you feel negative energy beginning to surge:

- **This has nothing to do with me**. Another person's behavior, success, reward, or good fortune has nothing to do with you. You most likely gain nothing or lose anything due to their situation. Even in cases in which we feel we "lost" due to someone else's "win" it is probably not an accurate assessment. In many of these situations, it probably wasn't ours to lose.

- **Why am I irritated?** Often, our disappointment or irritation stems from our view of our self or our life. We feel that we deserve something more than someone else. Is it jealousy? Is it a sense of justice? It doesn't make any difference. The most likely cause is petty, below you, and non-productive.

- **I am blessed**. Still struggling? Count your blessings. What is good in your life? What is good about you? Make a list. Focus on YOU and quit worrying about someone else.

- **Am I holding on to something?** In some cases, we are treated unjustly. Perhaps the circle of concern encroaches, and we get hurt or receive poor treatment at the hands of someone else. Let it go. Yes. Let it go. We only hurt our self when we hold on to an indignity. Harboring thoughts of revenge, getting "even," or the negative energy of anger bring stress, frustration, and angst into our world and the world of those around us. Whatever it is, let it go.

- **What can I do?** If the situation is within your circle of influence, then by all means take constructive action. Cast a vote, confront it, seek to make a difference, be the change you want to see. Often, we'll realize that we are focusing externally rather than concentrating on being the best version of our self.

Ultimately, we are only in control of one thing: ourselves. When we give in to our internal "control freak," we fool ourselves into believing we have a disproportionate influence on the world around us and end up disappointed. When we focus on our situation relative to that of someone else, we set ourselves up for doubt and resentment. When we "rage against the machine," we are screaming impotence in a big, broad world rather than focusing on our more immediate world over which we have some degree of influence.

Adversity, Gratitude, and Possibility

Sweet are the uses of adversity, Which, like the toad, ugly and venomous, Wears yet a precious jewel in his head; And this our life, exempt from public haunt, Finds tongues in trees, books in the running brooks, Sermons in stones, and good in everything.
—William Shakespeare, As You Like It

As I consider this Thanksgiving holiday, I'm struck by the curious intersection of gratitude and the ongoing challenges of life. We spend so much effort trying to manage and avoid struggles, yet they are integral to our ability to appreciate the gifts in our life. No one wants heartache, yet we know it is coming. No one seeks loss, yet all of us must endure it. Nobody welcomes pain, yet it is the whetstone for much of the joy that appears in our lives. How can something so painfully inevitable also be so vital to our growth and development as human beings? Here are some famous thoughts on adversity:

- *Strength rejoices in the challenge*. (*Virtus Tentamine Gaudet*) The motto of Hillsdale College.

- *That which does not kill us makes us stronger*. —Friedrich Nietzsche

- *Every adversity, every failure, every heartache carries with it the seed of an equal or greater benefit*. —Napoleon Hill

- *You don't develop courage by being happy in your relationships every day. You develop it by surviving difficult times and challenging adversity.* —Epicurus

- *If we will be quiet and ready enough, we shall find compensation in every disappointment.* —Henry David Thoreau

Now consider gratitude. Our forefathers felt that it was so important that they created a national holiday to celebrate it. Continually highlighted, gratitude remains a cornerstone of our social ethos:

- Gratitude works like a muscle. Take time to recognize good fortune, and feelings of appreciation can increase. (*Diana Kapp, Wall Street Journal*, 12/23/13)

- Cultivating an "attitude of gratitude" has been linked to better health, sounder sleep, less anxiety and depression, high long-term satisfaction with life and kinder behavior toward others. (*John Tierney, New York Times*, 11/21/11)

Our capacity, and need, to give thanks goes hand-in-hand with the various struggles we face during our lifetime. Time often gives us perspective on the struggles so we can recall the benefits of pushing through, surviving, enduring. What are you thankful for? Chances are that it comes directly from or through a challenging experience. It was earned. A few examples:

- **Relationships**: strong relationships are forged through shared challenges, external or internal. The inevitable challenges of a long-term relationship will either strengthen those bonds or tear them apart.

- **Health**: we will all face challenges with our health. If you are feeling grateful for your health today, it is likely that you earned it through enduring a setback or working hard to remain healthy.

- **Education**: it is only attained through discipline and time, both of which present challenges.

- **Freedom**: to value this, you must appreciate how it was earned and how it has been maintained. Otherwise, it is completely abstract.

- **Things**: if you are thankful for your possessions, you know what it took to acquire them. There are challenges and sacrifices along the way, and your appreciation of what you have is forged in that process.

- **Success**: I include this general bucket because it is completely personal to your situation. Defined by you, it is the best example of the intersection between gratitude and struggle. If you are thankful for your level of success, you will keenly know what you had to overcome to attain it.

My list is by no means exhaustive, but it illustrates my point. Thanksgiving is about recognizing the struggles, the adversity, that brought you to this point. Now, there is one more element to this story: possibility. If Thanksgiving is the rearview mirror to those moments when we pushed through adversity, possibility is the crystal ball for the ones yet to come. Possibility is hope for what might be.

As much as I am thankful for the gifts of my life to this point and in this moment, possibility is what keeps me going. Hope. Hope for my children and all they might accomplish with their lives. Hope for moments yet to be experienced. Hope for a world that presents more challenges than I can understand and more potential for good than I'll ever comprehend. The possibility of tomorrow seems endless. This Thanksgiving, I am betting on possibility. That blind faith in a tomorrow that will shape us into what we are to be and take us where we are supposed to go.

Trigger Creativity with Tension

I think what makes the work worth talking about is tension and fear. There is tension because we are simultaneously doing something that might work and something that might not work. And living with both of those things at the same time is very difficult for most people.
—Seth Godin

The Edge

In his audio presentation, "Leap First: Creating Work That Matters," Seth Godin challenges our thinking as he pushes us to "ship our art" into the world. One of his segments presents the notion of tension as a mechanism for creativity. Godin argues that our best work is done on the edge between "this might work" and "this might not work."

Think about that for a moment. Godin challenges us to embrace tension rather than avoid or eliminate it. Our natural inclination is to reduce tension. We want to run away from it. However, pushing through tension, working at it, and letting it unfold yields our best results.

Tough Decisions

Consider a tough decision you may be facing. From your vantage point, there is no right answer as none of your options are appealing. As you consider the facts of the situation and waffle back and forth, it is draining and frustrating. In this situation, our tendency is to relieve the tension as quickly as possible. We make a call and push forward. Or we make no call and retreat from any decision. We abdicate.

Decisiveness Versus Endurance

I am a big believer in being decisive. We never have all of the facts, but there is a time to make a decision and push forward. However, there is tremendous benefit to enduring the tension to make a *better* decision. Time is one element, but other things can be happening as well. We may have one more conversation that brings a fresh perspective. The morning shower may foster one brilliant idea. Someone else may decide to relieve their tension and open the door for us. *Enduring the tension as it unfolds can change everything.*

The tension is uncomfortable, but pushing through it can yield our best work. That edge heightens our senses, challenges us to be more. We will lean into it, or we will retreat from it? It is a choice. It is YOUR choice. This isn't masochism but an opportunity for enlightenment and improvement. Tension gives us the chance to rise to the occasion and stand apart. Choosing to endure it empowers and emboldens us.

Be In-*Tension*-Al

The next time you feel the tension in a situation, stop for a moment and consider it. Rather than seeking to relieve it by speaking first, making a snap decision, running from it, or abdicating responsibility, embrace it for a few moments. Deliberately holding the tension feels incredibly unnatural so you will have to be very determined. However, on that edge, in that moment, you may feel something else. You may recognize that pushing beyond the tension reveals another path, another idea, or simply relieves you of a fear that you held dear. Intentionally walking through the tension might take you toward something new and surprising.

Give Your Best Every Day

Half-heartedness is a disease to which we all succumb. If you choose to invest your time in an endeavor, is it worth your best? If not, why are you doing it? Give your best every day.

Effort and Generosity: Watch Closely Now

Watch closely now. You'll observe a curious exchange of energy
Are you a figment of my imagination
Or I one of yours?
Watch closely now
Are you watching me now?
—Kris Kristofferson, "Watch Closely Now"

Not long ago, I watched Barbara Streisand's 1976 film, *A Star is Born*. The movie tells the story of the relationship between a rock star facing the decline of his career and a rising star he chooses to help in her ascent. The movie features a collection of painfully self-destructive decisions mixed with the fiery passions of the two artists.

The feature song of the movie is a rock anthem sung by Kris Kristofferson entitled "Watch Closely Now." The lyrics of the song encapsulate the entire movie and are brought to life by the powerfully throaty voice of Kristofferson. Now, you are asking, why is he writing about a song in a forty-year-old movie?

For over forty years, I've been fascinated by this song. The entire soundtrack is very well done, but this song has resonated with me since I first heard it in 1976. On the surface, it is a catchy tune worth playing loudly in the car (or on your blue Panasonic cassette player!). But even before I could really understand, I sensed there was more to it.

Now, with a bit more perspective, I find myself intrigued by the underlying message: *Watch closely, I'll show you, I'll help you get where you want to be, I'm here, you're not alone, we can do this.* It is an offer, an invitation to walk together toward something more.

I recently spoke to a room full of professionals about the path to your best work in your peak years. I like to open this talk with the following statement: *"Your purpose in this world is to be the best you can possibly be...for yourself and the world around you."*

There is a powerful connection between effort and generosity. When we put the effort into being our best, we spark a cascade of inward and outward benefits. For ourselves, we engage our faculties to their fullest and affirm our sense of satisfaction stemming from giving our best effort. For those around us, the impact multiplies, not only for those who directly receive the benefits of our efforts, but others they may impact and for those watching. What are the side effects of your best effort? Here are a few:

- Direct impact—like an athlete performing at his or her best during a contest, our best efforts help us and our teammates win.

- Inspiration—when we give our best in a game, at the office, at home, in our church, at our school, or on whatever field we are playing, it inspires others to be more and do more.

- Education—our best efforts show others the way.

- Entertainment—remember the last time you watched an athlete perform at his or her peak? It was not only inspiring but entertaining as well. An element of joy awaits those around you when you give your best.

Giving your best is an act of generosity...to you and to everyone around you. Because most of us are not performing in front of live audiences in a play, ballet, athletic contest, or some other highly visible activity, we often feel that no one is watching. Believe me, people are watching and care in more ways than you realize. If you have a leadership position, your best efforts are very important to those around you. Guess what? We all hold leadership positions: in our families, in our churches, at our schools, in our clubs, and even in our non-management positions. Your efforts are important; your best efforts are gifts.

Finally, a major part of being your best self for the world around you is helping others become the best versions of themselves. Our job is to show others the way by our example. When we give our best, we inspire ourselves and other to be more, to do more. As William Danforth says in his book, *I Dare You*, "Our most valuable possessions are those which can be shared without lessening, those which, when shared, multiply." *Watch closely now. Are you watching me now?* Ask yourself: who is watching me and what am I showing them? Then provide an example worth emulating.

Your Best Is Age Independent

Those younger often look my way,
With pity looks to give
Yet this old body doesn't mean I am dying,
But rather, that I have lived
—Emily Nelson

My wife, Sally, loves the elderly. She always has. From the earliest moments of our relationship, I can remember the fondness she felt for her grandparents and the many stories that sprang from a youth spent in their presence. With time, I discovered that her affection for these long lives ran even deeper. Drawn to their stories, their wizened faces, and the slower pace of a point in life at which they no longer hurry to the next arrival, she finds joy in their company, in the people they are now, and the way they see the world. She *sees* them as people of beauty and worth.

One of her favorite movie directors is Robert Redford. She likes to describe the deliberate pace of his movies and the way his stories patiently unfold. I think this really captures the essence of her appreciation: she likes to see the stories patiently unfold. Like her own references to her grandparents, and now parents, she relishes their journeys and the reflections they cast of lives lived with meaning and value.

On a recent trip to northern California, we had the chance to slow down a bit and savor the natural beauty. From the antique furnishings in the little studio in which we stayed to the timelessly beautiful and rugged coastline, then beyond to ancient forests of massive redwoods, and finally the many fascinating people we encountered, she was always quick to point out what she described as the "beautifully old." I was immediately struck by her reflection.

Our cast-away world of cheap goods, perpetual consumption, and blistering pace often leaves little room for the old, used, worn, or depleted. We gather our detritus in neatly organized containers for recycling or unceremonious dumping in landfills and then fill our storage facilities with items we no longer use but feel compelled to keep. In many ways, our consumption mentality extends to the oldest members of our society as we herd them into facilities while looking for ways to better manage the challenges of their health, mental condition, or mobility more cost effectively.

As I age, my definition of "old" continues to evolve, and ages that once seemed ancient now appear quite young. A recent conversation with a retired man in his sixties reminded me of this as he described the difficulty of engaging with a world that didn't seem particularly interested in his services or capabilities. Even with an amazingly accomplished professional life, this individual had found that his age was an impediment to finding meaningful work. One might argue in a macroeconomic fashion about job trends, skill sets, globalization, and other broad concepts, but they have little meaning to the individual seeking ways to be productive without recommitting to entirely new careers or even full-time work.

Beautifully old. The expression still echoes across my mind. It implies value, worth, grace, and impact. Whether one considers old to be forty, sixty, or eighty makes little difference. There is beauty in aging and value in what it offers to those not yet there. Beautifully old suggests more than feeling of loss for what once was as it reminds us of what is now: weathered, wrinkled, worn, wise, gloriously alive, and valuable.

We all have the opportunity to be our best, to reach our peak, in any phase of life. In fact, we are called to do so. Part of being our best is helping those around us be their best. Whether employees, friends, loved ones, or *strangers*. We make the most difference when we pour all of ourselves into the world around us, giving our best every day. This could be charity, but it doesn't have to be. Our greatest gift could be the success we achieve that pulls others along with us, gives others around us purpose, or enables us to show others an example worth emulating.

I challenge you to recognize the beautifully old in the world around you. You may find it easy to appreciate beautifully old architecture or natural settings. Bring that appreciation to the people in your life who deserve it. *See* them and take a moment to consider what that means. Then step into the best version of yourself by deciding what you might do to make a difference.

Recognize Your Best

All your life, other people will try to take your accomplishments away from you. Don't you take them away from yourself.
—Michael Crichton, The Lost World

The Nature of Humility

Humility is a very tricky thing. In one sense, it captures the essence of being modest and understated. In another sense, it suggests that we take a low view of our own value. In general, we appreciate humble behavior in others. We respect humility as an opposing position to the offensiveness of hubris. A large part of the traditional American ethos revolves around the notion of being a hard-working, God-fearing group of people who must always exercise humility because who we are and what we have is a gift.

The Danger of Humility

Like so many other positive traits, humility at its extreme becomes a weakness. Why? Because it blinds us to our real value and the impact we have on the world around us. Taken to its far edge, humility restrains our potential as it whispers that your success is a gift and implies that perhaps you did not earn it. This narrative has the effect of convincing us to underestimate what we might accomplish.

Gratitude and Gifts

Wait a minute, shouldn't we be thankful for our gifts? Isn't gratitude a critical part of the fabric of the joy in our lives? Absolutely! However, this is where being humble can tip insidiously into the danger zone. You see, by embracing our good fortune as a gift, we open the door to the word "deserve." As soon as "deserve" enters the picture, we create a value measure around what we have done or are doing. If you are experiencing success as a gift, then the only way to deserve it is to be humble and appreciative. You don't earn a gift. If you aren't humble, perhaps the gift will be taken away.

The Blind Spot

Obviously, this isn't a conscious conversation with yourself. You may absolutely believe that you are working hard and earning every bit of your success. However, if you have difficulty balancing the tension between humility and hubris, you begin to fall into the comfort zone of underplaying your strengths. You tend to minimize your success, your impact, and your potential. You begin to doubt your effect. Ultimately, you create a blind spot where you have difficulty seeing how others perceive you and all the things of which you are capable. This is the ultimate loss because we can miss tremendous possibilities when we are blind to our impact on the people around us.

Embracing the Tension

Granted, hubris may be even more dangerous, but the challenge is to find some comfort in the tension between the two. We have to embrace our talents, even if they are gifts, and not view them through the lens of "deserved" but through the lens of "potential for impact." Seeing ourselves clearly and honestly assessing our potential for impact on those around us sets the stage for magic to happen. We begin to look for ways to deploy our strengths and possibilities present themselves.

The Fine Line

How do we walk the fine line between humility and hubris? There are no easy answers, and I think it will always be a challenge. Here are some ideas that might help:

- **Accept and embrace the tension between humility and hubris**. Our instinct is to retreat from tension. Recognize that it will be there and work to accept it.

- **Look at your gifts as tools**. If you accept that you have gifts, then you can balance the tension by viewing them and using them as a means to make a difference. If you are charismatic, use that gift to inspire others. If you are analytical, use that gift to help those who struggle with concrete planning. If you have a lot of money, use it in ways that make a difference either through charity or by creating jobs through your ongoing success.

- **Use your gifts to their maximum potential**. This helps offset the "deserved" challenge. Be honest about your capabilities and look for ways to grow to reach your potential. This will help pull you out of the "too humble" zone while reconciling accomplishment with purpose.

- **Ask for feedback**. Getting honest feedback on how others view you, where you might have blind spots, and how you might do more with your talents can open up a whole new world of possibility. This also works the other way. If you get feedback that you come across arrogantly in certain situations, there might be a disconnect between your self-perception and what you project.

- **Self-Assessments**. There are many great tools available to help you think through your gifts and capabilities. These tools make it easier for you to be honest about what you have and consider how you might best apply it.

- **Keep the gratitude, lose the doubt**. I am a true believer in maintaining an attitude of gratitude. We all have many gifts for which we should be thankful. Be thankful and quit worrying about whether or not you deserve them. If you don't think you deserve them, then DO something with those gifts that affirms that you were the absolute right person to receive them.

Humility: Strength and Weakness

I still believe that humility can be a strength. It is an endearing trait that fosters goodwill and trust. However, if we let it blind us to our true potential or allow it to convey a sense that we doubt ourselves, it can undermine our leadership and hold us back. Be aware of these dangers and vigilant for the blind spots. There you will find the tension as you walk the path to your greatest impact.

Show Others the Way

All employees have an innate desire to contribute to
something bigger than themselves.
—Jag Randhawa

Many years ago, I worked for a young, high-growth company providing information technology services to corporations. I believe my employee number was 610. The founder of the company was a dynamic individual who had big dreams and serious determination. Like many high-powered founders, he floated between manic obsessive devil and charismatic angel, often able to cross the distance between the two within the same conversation. He inspired fear and awe while communicating a clear vision, a clear sense of value to our customers, and a clear understanding of what it takes to build a high-growth company.

In today's world of "engagement" and the host of buzzwords surrounding organizational development, I often think of my time in that company. Before selling, we had about fifteen hundred employees who were very engaged, very focused, and very passionate about their work and their company. We didn't know what a Millennial was, though there was a bit of talk about Generation X…or was it Y? It didn't matter. We were on a mission and everyone was engaged.

Though it seems like a long time ago (over twenty years), much of the experience still resonates with me and I find myself repeating many of my former employer's mantras in my mind. Today, we spend so much time trying to figure out how to engage employees, create meaningful work environments, and manage the newest generation (which is always different in a negative way from the one before) when things are really pretty simple. We confuse culture with purpose and get lost in a host of creative distractions to try and delight our workforce (pick your favorite Silicon Valley office culture gimmick: Ping-Pong tables, oxygen bars, dogs at work, etc.).

How did that high-growth company mentioned above do it? Our founder started with three guiding questions that all employees ask:

1. Where are we going?

2. How will we get there?

3. What's in it for me?

Then he answered them in a cohesive vision:

1. Purpose/Direction: A five-year window to a liquidity event and stock options for employees.

2. Focus: A set of highly differentiated services in a targeted niche.

3. Opportunity: The chance to grow financially, personally, and professionally along the way.

Next, he provided a clear set of organizational values. What was important to us?

1. Do the right thing, every time.

2. Excellence in everything we do.

3. The growth and development of our people.

Of course, the lists above are meaningless without execution. In this case, the company was able to execute. Not only did we speak in terms of the items above, we were measured on them, we were held accountable to them, and we believed in them. The expression "cult-like" comes to mind, but it was quite effective and didn't seem too terribly weird at the time.

I'm sure my experience was not unique. There were many successful companies before and many since, all with their own unique culture and path to success. Yes, market timing and service set made a difference in our ultimate success, but the underlying principles fueled and reinforced everything we did that led to that success. It is still a good model for today when we continue to ask how to engage our employees.

As I look back, I see three key factors that truly stand out and they weren't about pay, the appearance of our office furniture, or any other gimmick:

- We all felt like we were part of, and contributing to, something bigger than ourselves.

- We all felt like we were on a winning team.

- Leadership did what it said it would do.

We didn't know anything about being engaged but we were definitely bought-in. Everyone in that organization had a greater sense of purpose. What we were doing was making a difference. Sure, we wanted to get paid and have fun doing our work, but the real drivers were much more profound. It was a true work-hard, play-hard culture and the fun came in daily steps toward the attainment of a shared vision. My conclusion? Quit worrying about coddl…er, I mean, motivating Millennials or any other generation with gimmicks or tchotchkes. Just give them something to believe in, a great team to be on, and a pathway to shared success. Then, follow through on the vision you paint. Every individual is called to make a difference in the world around them. Each of us is called to be the best version of our selves. Then, as employers, business owners, and leaders, we are called to do our best to create an environment in which people can accomplish their basic purpose.

Trust Others to Be Their Best

Trust is the highest form of human motivation.
It brings out the very best in people.
—Stephen R. Covey

For the last several days, the concept of empowerment has been rolling around in my head, and I keep getting glimpses of an equation. It is more of a proof. Forgive the mathematical reference but bear with me for a moment. The outline below is organization-centric.

1. Success equals a profitable, growing business.

2. A profitable, growing business depends on having a collection of empowered employees.

3. To empower employees requires that leadership trusts them.

4. For employees to accept empowerment, they must trust their leaders.

5. Therefore, to be successful, leaders must create an environment of trust.

Simple enough, right? Empower the members of our team and they'll do great things! Of course, it isn't quite that simple. True empowerment is built on trust, and trust is a very complicated thing. And yet trust *is also very simple*. True trust is not something we give, it is something we earn. It is built one action, one word, one step at a time over a period of time. It is also something that is lost in an instant.

What is trust? Trust is relying on someone else to do or not do something. Trust is having faith in another person. Trust is depending on someone else. Trust exposes us to some level of risk, from mild disappointment to catastrophic betrayal. Trust is built over time and lost in a moment.

> True trust is not something we give, it is something we earn.

What does trust have to do with empowerment? To truly empower your team, you must trust them enough to fail, or you aren't trusting them enough to succeed. Let me repeat: to truly empower your team, you must trust them enough to fail, or you aren't trusting them enough to succeed.

What a frightening concept! We talk a lot about empowerment. We intuitively understand that it is necessary for our organizations to thrive. Yet we still struggle with empowering our people. We could go into many psycho-social directions with this, but I don't want to address control issues in this post.

Building Trust

If you want to truly empower your team, to help them be their best for themselves and for your organization, you've got to trust them. Understanding how trust works and how it is built will *empower* you to *empower* them. Here are three steps to trusting your team:

1. Start small to trust big.

2. Give progressive responsibility.

3. Buffer appropriately.

Start Small to Trust Big. Since trust is built through experience, the first step is to give individuals the chance to fail or succeed. The key is to start small. "Whoever can be trusted with very little, can also be trusted with very much." Give her a chance for small wins so she can demonstrate to you, and to herself, how well she can perform. This process builds confidence for both of you and begins steadily building the trust necessary to progress.

Give Progressive Responsibility. Confidence and trust move in parallel directions for you and for your team members. The small successes aggregate into increasing levels of trust. Giving someone additional responsibility or higher risk tasks/projects increases his confidence, shows that you trust him, and gives you a better idea of his capabilities and capacity. Conversely, if you aren't giving progressive responsibility, it sends a message that you don't trust him or are not confident in his abilities to do more. Intentional or not, the message will be sent.

Buffer Appropriately. We all have different risk tolerances. To build trust, you need to understand yours and your team members' risk threshold. To build trust, there must be an opportunity to fail. However, catastrophic failure is not good for anyone and you need to buffer appropriately. This is not backstopping. When we backstop, we are in effect assuming responsibility.

To build trust, there must be accountability and true opportunity to fail (or at least make mistakes). On the other hand, buffering is not putting a team member in a situation where failure is fatal, i.e., "If you don't close this deal, we are going out of business." Very few of us will perform optimally under these conditions. Buffering allows you to mitigate your risk while giving your employee the chance to succeed, or fail, in bigger ways—non-catastrophically.

The Other Side

There is another side to empowering your team. They must accept it. How do you get your team to accept the empowerment you want to give? **They must trust you**. You might ask, "Why wouldn't they trust me?" Let me count the ways...

- Not following through on commitments.

- Not honoring secrets.

- Not "managing up" when disagreement occurs.

- Gossip.

- Dishonesty—even in the small things.

- Treatment of others: customers, employees, family.

Remember, trust is a two-way street. Everything you say and do increases or decreases how much your team trusts you. Do you do what you say you're going to do in the little and the big things? Do you trust them enough to allow them to fail? Do you give them the tools, direction, and support they need to succeed when you give them an assignment? Do you look at mistakes as learning opportunities? Are you consistent? Are you emotional? These things add up—in one direction or the other.

Ultimately, for your team to accept empowerment, you must convince them that failure is not fatal. How do you accomplish this?

- **Be clear in defining success and failure.** The worst-case scenario should never be catastrophic.

- **Communicate that giving progressive responsibility is intentional.** It affirms that you see a path and that you are deliberately assigning difficulty by your measure of their capabilities.

- **Do what you say you're going to do.** When bumps in the road appear, be steady, be supportive, be consistent. Your integrity and follow-through will build your employee's trust in you and in herself. This is particularly true for little things. We almost always underestimate how they add up.

- **Celebrate wins and losses.** Okay, I know we don't really want to celebrate failures and mistakes. However, lessons learned in failures will bring you closer to the next win. Finding a way to acknowledge that and turn the mistake into an opportunity will go a long way toward reinforcing your message: I trust you. I buy in. I believe you can do it. We are in this together.

Conclusion

My conclusion? To be successful, we need to empower our teams, and true empowerment is trusting them enough to fail. When we give a person enough latitude to fail, we say, "I trust you. I believe in you. I've got your back."

By exposing us, and them, to the possibility of failure, we are empowering them to succeed through being the best version of themselves. We are giving them the chance to grow by allowing them to take responsibility and be accountable for a result. This empowerment translates into the "flywheel effect" and an increase in organizational momentum independent of our direct effort. It is a powerful multiplier and creates a win for all involved. Remember, trust → empowerment → success. Looks like the right formula to me.

Limits Can Help Us Be Our Best

Our problem as Americans is that we resist the very idea of limits, regarding limits of all sorts as temporary and regrettable impositions on our lives.
—Parker J. Palmer

Can you remember the dot.com crash of 2000? The "irrational exuberance" of investors in the late 1990s led to a string of catastrophic company failures as the dot.com house of cards came crashing down. For those of us in and around some of those companies in the late 1990s, it was amazing to behold. Money was being invested in myriad business models as the hunger for anything Internet-related built to a fever pitch.

The story seemed to be the same for so many: raise an obscene amount of money and then spend all of it on wild offices, Super Bowl advertising, and almost anything else that defied traditional start-up thinking. The sense was that the rules of the market and business had fundamentally changed; a new gold rush had emerged, and everyone was determined to cash in. Then, as quickly as it started, it all ended.

Though there were many reasons for the bursting of the dot.com bubble, I mostly remember the unfettered spending of so many companies that raised enormous amounts of money. Perhaps even more detrimental than poor business models or even macroeconomic pressures was the overabundance of money for these start-ups. There were no limits. There was no discipline. Why? Because they had so much funding that they didn't have to be resourceful or focused. Until they did, and then it was too late.

In America, we are obsessed with our personal freedoms. Nothing angers us faster than someone else trying to constrain us. This fiercely independent streak has served us well, and we defend it aggressively. However, like most things, too much of a good thing turns it into a bad thing. The best example of this is with our children. What happens to children with too much freedom? They become spoiled and entitled. They expect to get their way and throw fits when they don't. As parents, some of our greatest gifts to our kids are the limits we place on them. When we say no, we are showing them love by caring enough to do the hard work of disappointing them. Kids thrive within constraints.

Which brings me to my point: there is power in constraints. Limitations empower us by giving us direction and forcing us to be resourceful. We see this time and again in our personal and professional lives. Many of the best businesses are boot-strapped, which forces discipline and focus when they are testing the market and figuring out how to make everything work. The best students work within timelines, material, and structure. The best employees work well with clear expectations and constraints. Is this because they are being told what to do? No, it's because their constraints give them direction and demand the ingenuity to figure things out within those limits.

Limitations empower us by giving us direction and forcing us to be resourceful.

Properly applied, our limits empower us to do more and be more. Perhaps it is the challenge of being underfunded that pushes us to be more creative. It might be the determination we feel to push back on the rules that drives us to some greater accomplishment. Perhaps it is a more elemental defiance triggered by external constraints that drives us to new heights. Whatever the motivator, our constraints play a key part in enabling us to be our best.

Wait a minute! You may ask, "How can you talk about limits in a book centered on pushing us to be more, to be our best?" It is true that the world is adept at reminding us of what we can't do. We are very good at listening to that message and further limiting ourselves by fear and doubt. However, there is power in our constraints as well as opportunity.

The power is in what our limitations require of us: focus, discipline, creativity, grit. The opportunity lies in the fact that, by limiting us in some fashion, our constraints help us to be our best. As time goes on, those limitations fade as we grow into the next version of our self and realize that, more than holding us back, they freed us to become something more.

Seek Goodness Every Day

Do not act as if you were going to live ten thousand years. Death hangs over you. While you live, while it is in your power, be good.
—*Marcus Aurelius*

A headline appeared on LinkedIn the other day saying that a set of laws caused a medical provider to commit fraud. Though I wholeheartedly agree that the complexity of our laws leads to varying levels of non-compliance and that it is easy to get tripped up in the tangled web, there is often a fundamental problem with how we approach laws and the agencies enforcing them. The problem runs deeper—it's not just laws and regulations, it's how we seek to improve our position.

We live in a world in which everyone is trying to "game" the system. We seek advantages and shortcuts in every imaginable situation, sometimes hiding behind the way laws, rules, regulations, comp plans, contracts, etc., are written. Such is our legal system and the processes that support it. As participants in this world, we tend to get lost in the argument rather than focusing on the intent. Sometimes, the intent doesn't even matter as we twist and turn within the nuances of language and semantics. What was it the dad said in the movie *Clueless* so many years ago? "It's not what you earn, it's what you argue."

As I considered that LinkedIn headline and the hundreds of other daily headlines describing fraud and myriad other forms of law-breaking behavior, I wondered aloud why we make it so complex. We tend to get so lost in our rationalization mechanisms that we lose sight of the most basic elements of our being. Rather than focusing on taking advantage of the systems that govern our lives, what would happen if we started by seeking goodness?

I'm not talking about being "right" or "correct," nor I am I referring to the quality of a particular action or thought in terms of being effective. I'm referring to "good" in its most moral sense. We might describe a good person as exhibiting the traits of kindness, consideration, prudence, generosity, and forgiveness. We might say that good people observe the Golden Rule: treat others as you want to be treated. The essence of goodness might be captured by describing what it is not: good people don't lie, cheat, steal, or hurt others. When we use such words, what is "good" doesn't seem to be so ambiguous.

A recent discussion with a friend regarding a contract reminded me of this. The conversation started with his description of some clauses in an agreement and his desire to do some things that could potentially conflict with them. The answers weren't clear. We discussed the implications in several different scenarios and how the other party might react, finally getting to a point at which we were debating the legal arguments. At that point, I realized we were focused in the wrong direction. I asked my friend, "What was the intent of your agreement?" My point was: "You are bigger than this. You are feeling hesitations for a reason. You are a good person. Go to them and talk about what you want to do. Seek goodness."

> Rather than focusing on taking advantage of the systems that govern our lives, what would happen if we started by seeking goodness?

Yes, I know. The world is not black and white. Not everyone shares the same moral code. Sometimes the situation dictates certain behaviors that we might normally call immoral or not "good." Whatever. You know what I mean. Most of us are not dealing with daily decisions of life and death on a battlefield or living in such destitution that our only choice is to steal. In most cases, we are way past survival. We choose good or not in much, much smaller circumstances. Often, many times in a day.

What happens when we seek goodness? We apply powerful traits of empathy, caring, and consideration. We look for ways to forgive. We work for the betterment of other people. We try to understand intentions and give others the benefit of the doubt. We speak honestly, act honorably, and lift those around us with our integrity. We work for transactions that benefit all involved and listen to our conscience when it warns of occasions that compromise our goodness. Seeking goodness elevates us and the world around us.

Perhaps you feel that I'm suggesting we all put on our rose-colored glasses? Turn a blind eye to the ugliness and dishonesty of our world and skip obliviously happy into our day? No, I'm not suggesting obliviousness. Quite the contrary. I'm suggesting powerful intention. I'm advocating deliberate effort to seek goodness in yourself and in others. I'm suggesting that if you seek goodness, and live goodness, you will find it more often than not.

By the way, this is not a recipe for self-protection—you will be hurt, disappointed, and frustrated with others who don't share your approach. However, if you seek goodness and bring goodness to the world, you will find the contented joy of moving toward the best version of yourself. You will find the satisfaction of living honorably and sleeping soundly. You will find the fulfillment of knowing you have elevated those around you directly through your efforts and indirectly through your example. Sure, go ahead and argue the nuances of a clause. Just seek goodness first.

Doing Your Best Can Be Exhausting; Do It Anyway

I was blessed with the opportunity to coach youth athletics over a twelve-year period while my kids were in grade school and middle school. Basketball, softball, and soccer filled every spare moment of our evenings and week-ends. It was gloriously challenging, frustrating, and fulfilling... often simultaneously. During this time, I encountered many talented athletes, a few of whom went on to play in college. These young stars have been endlessly inspirational for me.

> To lift your team sometimes requires that you "spend" all you have: physically, emotionally, and spiritually.

Many years ago, a young lady who I had formerly coached was competing in a contest and was having an amazing game. Defensively and offensively, she was everywhere, and her performance lifted the team to success. After the game, I congratulated her on an amazing effort. She gave a little smile, crinkled her forehead, and said, "Thank you. It was exhausting."

Her comment didn't strike me as odd...I was certain she was exhausted after a long, demanding game. However, the expression she shared when she made the comment indicated something deeper. Not long after that, I saw her at another contest, a game in which she played well but nothing like the game referenced above. This time, her team lost. After the game, I asked her if she realized that she had the talent to lift her entire team when she called on it. With no hint of surprise, she said "Thank you" and went on to tell me that she knew she didn't play her absolute best and sometimes struggled to "go there" because it takes "so much out of her."

Before that moment, I never really understood what it took to be a star athlete, the person able to carry his/her team to victory in the most challenging moments. As I think back to that conversation, I realize that physical fatigue, though certainly present, had little to do with her exhaustion. To be your best, to perform at your peak, to give something your all, demands that you pour yourself into it. To lift your team sometimes requires that you "spend" all you have: physically, emotionally, and spiritually. In some cases, it demands that you spend more than you have.

In our days in the office, at the hospital, in the classroom, on the road, at the store, at home, or wherever else we may spend our waking time, we are given the opportunity to show up, be present, and do our best. We are called to be the best version of our self. Is that what we are being? We often casually say "I did my best," sometimes as a justification for losing, forgetting, coming up short, or any number of other outcomes in which things didn't work out as expected.

The reality is that doing your best is no small feat. Our best effort, best performance, best attitude, best appearance, best preparation, and on and on, require tremendous effort. To be our best demands focus and exertion: physical, mental, and spiritual. It *is* exhausting.

Doing your best is exhausting. Do it anyway. The athlete I mentioned earlier went on to play in college on a scholarship, had many more wonderful and challenging experiences in her basketball career, graduated, jumped into her career, and is now building her family. The discipline of doing her best permeates everything in her life and fuels a joy that is pure and true. Along the way, she touched many, many lives and continues to do so. Was your best worth it? "Absolutely!" she replies.

We innately understand that doing our best can lead to success of various flavors. There is another benefit to doing your best: the pure, glorious satisfaction of having left everything you had on the field. Anyone who has exercised at their peak understands there is a joy at

> We often casually say "I did my best," sometimes as a justification for losing, forgetting, coming up short, or any number of other outcomes in which things didn't work out as expected.

depletion, at the edge. At the edge, even winning the contest become less important because, inside, the athlete knows that he/she has paid the price in putting everything into the effort and now feels the satisfaction of standing there, emptied and fulfilled. Performance of any sort presents a similar opportunity. When we execute and invest ourselves to our fullest, the joy of satisfaction must follow. Yes, we always want to win. But in this place, there is clear joy in the journey.

Doing your best demands something more from you. The amazing gifts and capabilities you have must be fully engaged if they are to bear fruit. Your best effort isn't doing what you *feel* **like doing in the moment. Your "best" is** not a relative term that is more on some days and less on others. Doing your best means that you are being all of which you are capable in that moment. It is a very tall order because you are capable of truly amazing things.

Don't lose heart. The good news is that living your best life doesn't mean you're exerting at peak levels in every second. Fortunately, most of us don't live in a world in which we've got to be running at peak exertion in every moment to survive. However, we must realize that being our best demands effort. Giving our best to our jobs and to the people around us will be exhausting. Do it anyway. The joy and satisfaction will follow.

Be Vulnerable Every Day

*Safety is a mirage. Security is ephemeral.
Our best life waits at the edges—scary places where we have the chance to
become something more. Be vulnerable every day.*

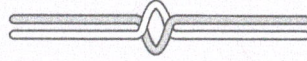

Finding Our Limits at the Edges

If I'm not saying to myself, "This might not work"…then I haven't pushed myself hard enough.
—Seth Godin

I absolutely love the quotation above. It captures the essence of any project worth doing and has been particularly applicable in my own entrepreneurial journey. It is the edge. That place we stand, facing the possible and experiencing the discomfort of the risk in leaping toward it. Age and experience don't matter—there is an edge for us at any stage of our life. At that edge, we realize that "this might not work."

At that edge lies vulnerability. The easy thing is to shrink from it. Retreat. Most of us have built a life of comfort. A life of safety. This doesn't mean we're satisfied or that we've stopped aspiring to more. Nor does it mean that we live risk-free. It means that we go to places we know, interact with people familiar to us, take jobs we're certain we can do, and make decisions that reinforce those comfortable, safe *feelings*. Our natural state is to move away from risk. Identify it. Manage it. Eliminate it. School, job, relationship, money…decision after decision, we aim for the comfortable place, the safe place. Well, at least it's the place we feel is most comfortable. The place that seems less risky.

Still, things seem to happen. We lose the comfortable job. Our long-term relationship ends. Our portfolio tanks. Tragedy strikes. @!#$ happens. So much for comfort. So much for safety. Yet, time and again, we move on. We recover. We push through. We lean in. If safety is never quite as safe as it appears, is it possible that the risks might not be as great as they seem?

A recent headline caught my eye: "Why Most People Will Never Succeed." I didn't bother reading it. There are a million reasons why someone might not succeed, but there are only two that truly matter: 1) the person didn't try or 2) the person chose the wrong success. If you define the right success for you based on your priorities, values, and the price you are willing to pay, then you will find it if you try. There is always success waiting for us if we are willing to recognize it. Sometimes, it looks different than we expected.

"This might not work" means that you are choosing to push yourself toward something that you might not reach. A success that is a stretch. Falling short doesn't necessarily mean failure, nor does it have to be the end. We almost always find something else along the way. Another version of success. A new discovery about our self. Perhaps a completely different perspective on why we started down the path to begin with. All this from simply stepping to the edge, accepting the risk of failure, and leaping anyway.

What might not work for you in the days ahead? Think about it and answer the question wholeheartedly. Because, on the flip side are those things that just might work for you. That crazy idea that you could never implement. The job opportunity that is so completely out of your league. A project that would have a huge impact on your company or not-for-profit and is simply impossible. The list is endless. What might you do if you knew that failure was impossible? THAT is the edge…and the opportunity.

By the way, that risk you see lying beyond the edge? It might be less than the risk of standing still—the unseen risk of a false sense of security. Feeling vulnerable doesn't necessarily mean the risks are greater. Find your own edge and then move beyond it. Who knows? It might just work.

In Defense of Imperfect Writing

Truly perfect is becoming friendly with your imperfections on the way to doing something remarkable.
—Seth Godin

WARNING: **If you are a grammar troll, you may find these heretical comments, unintentional grammatical errors, and accidental typos offensive. Proceed with caution.**

A recent *Harvard Business Review* post entitled "Stop Trying to Sound Smart When You're Writing" evoked a visceral response in me. It wasn't the topic or the points made. In fact, the author made some very valuable points on ways we all might improve our writing. What really struck me was the tone of the piece. A tone that the author tried to subdue with logical, even-tempered suggestions on the nuts and bolts of writing, but then released when she specified her "pet peeve"—using "methodology" when one should be using "method." These screeds on wise and proper writing always get to the "pet peeve," the word, phrase, or euphemism that really sets off the author's inner grammar troll.

Please don't misunderstand. I am all for making your writing as perfect as possible. After all, we all appreciate a finely tuned sentence that is clear, concise, and grammatically correct. If the sentence can also be touching, poetic, or beautiful in its artistic elegance, all the better. My "pet peeve" is the constant need in our society to identify everyone else's imperfections and seek to correct them. When we miss the message in another person's communication because we're too busy editing their language, everyone loses.

Let's take the cliché as an example. Here is the definition of cliché:

> A *cliché* (/ˈkliːʃeɪ/ or /klɪˈʃeɪ/) is an expression, idea, or element of an artistic work that has become overused to the point of losing its original meaning or effect, even to the point of being trite or irritating, especially when at some earlier time it was considered meaningful or novel.

In this case, we're talking about an expression or idea that at one time was considered meaningful or novel. Then, because so many people thought it meaningful or novel, the expression lost its appeal. In other words, we liked it so much and so often that we finally decided to stop liking it. Grammar trolls are famously aggressive with regard to clichés, hackneyed sayings, or trite expressions. Of course, "hackneyed" is often in the eye of the beholder, and though it may offend one person, it may resonate resoundingly with someone else.

What about grammar or spelling mistakes? Though the *Chicago Manual of Style* may be the final arbiter of good taste as it relates to proper writing, each of us judges one another on a relative scale with regard to grammar or spelling errors. Our personal scale is built completely on our sense of correctness and propriety with regard to the English language (or whatever language in which we are communicating). Therefore, if I am a poor speller, I may be far more tolerant of poor spelling from other people. Though poor spelling may reflect imperfect

In our quest to judge, we often miss the point and an opportunity to learn something.

communication and an imperfect grasp of the English language, it doesn't necessarily indicate poor ideas. In our quest to judge, we often miss the point and an opportunity to learn something.

There is another element to this argument. I referenced it earlier, and it is far more insidious. In our ongoing efforts to be right, find flaws, or be the one to have "seen it first," we are quick to criticize another human being. Our efforts aren't focused on constructively improving, tenderly supporting, or sincerely advising another so that he or she may grow to be his or her best. No, we are tearing down. We are humiliating. We are hurting another. And for what? The pride of being correct? The satisfaction of being the first to see the error? The self-congratulatory gratification of clearly being the superior human being in a particular interaction?

What is the point of our criticism? Few of us are professional critics. (Do we really need such a thing as a "professional critic?") When we get hung up in the flaws, attack someone's imperfection, or belittle the work of another simply because we can, then we are giving up a bit of our humanity in the process. We are lessening our self for no purpose. There is a reason that many fear to share an opinion, a piece of art, or a special talent: the price of vulnerability can be devastating.

So lose your grammar police badge. If a person's writing, hackneyed expressions, poor spelling, or incorrect grammar turn you off, just move on. If you feel that you can help them be a better writer, artist, professional, or human being, then by all means share your wisdom in the spirit of helping them improve. But consider your

> There is a reason that many fear to share an opinion, a piece of art, or a special talent: the price of vulnerability can be devastating.

motivations before you hit "submit." As the writer, the question to ask is: "Did you know what I meant?" Please, correct all the punctuation errors. Just don't lose the point in your quest for perfection.

And for those seeking to write or put their art into the world. Be prepared for the critics. There is no escape. Take what helps, ignore the rest, and work to improve your craft. It is as simple as that.

Art, Work, and Vulnerability

Art is the work of a human being—something a person does with generosity to touch someone else to make a change for the better.
—Seth Godin

What Is Art?

Thank you, Seth, for reminding us that we are all capable of making art, of touching someone else with our gifts.

When I published my first book, *Stones Across the River*, in November 2016, it was an exciting process that revealed many things to me about myself, the world of writing, and what it means to make art and bring it to market. Along the way, I've encountered many people with hopes, dreams, and gifts that are resting dormant, waiting to be brought to life.

Art can encompass anything we are doing to make a change for the better: our jobs in healthcare, the way we serve others in our day-to-day roles, how we make a meal or cafe latte, or any number of other acts of generosity in how we deploy our gifts to the world. The scope is broad, as are the talents we bring to the world.

The traditional view of art revolves around a work: a painting, a sculpture, a performance, a piece of music, etc. Of course, each of these can be a form of art, but just because someone puts pen to paper or paintbrush to canvas doesn't necessarily mean he is making art. One might be a great mass producer of replicas, but that person isn't bringing anything new, or generous, to the world.

The New Makers

My wife, Sally, and I recently attended the Country Living Fair in Columbus, OH. The fair was a collection of vendors selling a variety of crafts, antiques, foods, and other handmade items that seemed to generally fit into the "country chic" style made famous by Chip and Joanna Gaines on the HGTV show, *Fixer Upper.*

As we moved among the booths and displays, I was struck by the number of craftspeople selling handmade or artisan products. In this case, "artisan" is defined as low volume, specialty craft items that focus on quality and design. The variety was amazing.

Over the last few years, the appetite and availability of these specialty products has exploded. We have craft beer, artisan cocktails, farm-to-table restaurants, self-published authors, self-recording musicians, boutique hotels, and Etsy has brought us a whole new world of crafty, high-quality products that are quickly produced and often customizable.

Sure, the term "artisan" has been overused and hijacked for marketing purposes, but the demand for these products is strong, and as is the truth with most art, beauty and quality are in the eye of the beholder. The age of low-volume, high-quality, artisan goods is here, and Americans can't get enough of it.

What's driving these new makers? New tools, new distribution channels, and a new hunger for non-cookie cutter, healthier, and environmentally friendly products. In Indianapolis and across the country, the trend away from chain restaurants and toward locally owned, farm-to-table, and organic fare has opened new worlds for would-be restaurateurs and entrepreneurs. Hand-in-hand with this trend is the explosion of craft brewing, which seems to spawn a new brewery every day, with an amazingly cool name and label for incredibly creative mixtures of flavors and ingredients sold as the no-longer-mundane product we call beer.

Want to create a candle company? There are companies who will get you set up to produce your own soy candles. Want to publish a book? There are companies who will walk you through every step of getting your novel to market. Want to sell your handmade sweaters? Etsy and other online outlets provide easy access to an entire world of consumers looking for your artisan product.

For me, the trend is profound in a different way. As much as I love the artisan products, I really admire the new spirit of these businesses and the craftspeople behind them. In many cases, these artisan makers do not aspire to create a mega-company. For many of them, the trends, tools, and channels are simply an opportunity for them to do something they enjoy and possibly earn a living doing it. Most are probably not calling their products *art*, but they are certainly being generous in sharing their art with the rest of us.

Sharing Your Art Makes You Vulnerable

Whenever we put something out there, we expose ourselves to criticism, ridicule, and rejection. That is the nature, and necessity, of game day. To live fully and be all of which we are capable, we must put our art, our work, our craft, our effort on display. We must share it.

Sharing our gifts with the world, and therein becoming vulnerable, is essential to the realization of our best self. Asking someone to buy a product we made exposes us to rejection. Stepping on the field to test our mettle against an opponent risks the experience of losing. However, if we don't do it, we risk missing acceptance or the opportunity to win. There is no progress without vulnerability. There is no success without risk.

There are many talented artists out there who touch us with their amazing gifts and their beautiful works. Thank you for sharing. There are also many of us out there who have gifts we have not yet shared. Beautiful works that are waiting to be realized. What is holding you back? It is likely that most of us will never publish a best-seller, have our painting exhibited in an art museum, see our photographs in *National Geographic*, or sell our handmade furniture in a home store, but that doesn't change the fact that we've got a gift. We've got something to share. In fact, there may be an audience waiting for us to bring our art to market.

Choose Yourself

Most of us live our lives hoping someone will recognize our talents. We wait to be chosen. This is a lottery ticket mentality. We think: "Hopefully, I'll show up one day and they will pick my number." For me, writing and publishing my book was a decision to choose myself. In the process, I decided there is an opportunity to help others choose themselves, to help them find their audience and bring their art to market. The goal doesn't have to be to get rich or change careers or build a business. Perhaps sharing our art with a small group of people who care about it is enough. Perhaps the opportunity to make more of my art is a reward in itself. Perhaps the chance to share, the chance to experience, the chance to connect, and the chance to push our talents is worth the risk. You can't know until you make yourself vulnerable. Today is your opportunity, and your best work is waiting to be realized.

Be Passionate Every Day

The mass of men lead lives of quiet desperation.
—*Henry David Thoreau*

The very expression "quiet desperation" sends a chill down my back. The words evoke a visceral sense of being trapped, of looking out of a window upon a world in which we want to live but seem unable to join. Shakespearean tragedy comes to mind as I consider the potential results of a lifetime of quiet desperation. To counter the disease of quiet desperation, I would prescribe a daily dose of passion.

What happens when we wake up and face our day with a burning passion? There is a spring in our step. The annoyances of the morning wash away in the bright light of the day's possibilities. Passion fuels a desire to jump in, get busy, and make it happen. Game days are filled with the surge of competition, exertion, comradery, risk, and passion.

On the surface, passion for something seems obviously positive. What a gift to feel passionate toward something! However, there is risk with passion. We invest ourselves in our passions, and where we invest ourselves reveals our priorities. This is a place of exquisite vulnerability. Our passions express our most elemental drivers in billboard-like fashion: "THIS IS IMPORTANT TO ME!"

Whenever we give ourselves to something fully, we risk criticism. Whether on the field, on the stage, in the office, or on the page, our passions broadcast that we are all-in. When we are all-in on anything, we expose ourselves to the contempt of other human beings as well as the potential failures intrinsic to any worthy endeavor. Vulnerability goes hand in hand with passion.

Some choose to dim the bulb on the bright light of their passions. Keep a low profile, they think, so there is little risk of criticism. Others may choose to ignore passions and play it safe on the sidelines, half-heartedly cheering the other players racing the down the field. Still others may listen to those closest to them, not criticizing, but discouraging passion of any undesirable flavor. There are many ways to dampen these flames.

Passion, be it physical, emotional, or spiritual, is a critical element of game-day performance. Not uncontrolled, wanton fire, but focused energy toward a meaningful objective. The vulnerability brought on by passion is a necessary by-product, and it's *integral to its benefits*. When we open ourselves to passion, we open a direct channel to the most vulnerable recesses of our being, our very essence. This exposure is why the risks are so high, and also why the rewards can be so great. The danger of vulnerability takes us to the edge, and game day is all about edges.

As I write this, it seems a bit odd to include a piece on passion in the middle of a chapter on vulnerability. However, it is exactly this dichotomy that frames the edgy connection between the two. Our passions drive us, fuel us to invest our faculties in specific directions. There we find the exposure and the fulfillment that vulnerability provides. In the end, walking through our vulnerability toward our passions prepares us for the road beyond. On this side of quiet desperation, it can be daunting. Walk toward it anyway. Be passionate every day.

We All Hate to Lose

If you can keep your wits about you while all others are losing theirs, and blaming you. The world will be yours and everything in it, what's more, you'll be a man, my son.
—Rudyard Kipling, If

Nearing the end of my daughter's high school career, I attended a post-season high school football game. The chilly night and clear skies heralded a more profound change in the season. The stadium was brilliantly lit, allowing me to see the shadows of trees and partly fallen leaves just beyond the fences. Fans were colorfully adorned to represent their teams, and the hats, gloves, and cups of hot chocolate confirmed that we had crossed over into new temperature territory from earlier in the afternoon. I had met my youngest daughter and her friend for dinner just an hour before and then watched them drive off to the game, reminding me of yet another change in seasons. The night was replete with shifting tides.

In the stands, I sat with some old friends but recognized few of our fellow fans. I realized that our ten-year run as parents of students at this school was coming to an end. The realization wasn't really a sad one, more of an acknowledgment of the necessity of this transition…for all of us. As I watched the game, I felt strangely detached. The players were unfamiliar. The stakes weren't real for me. I wasn't invested. I was truly a spectator.

My detachment gave me a fresh perspective on the game. Nearby fans were yelling about bad calls and terrible officiating. All I saw were bad decisions, poor execution, or simply mistakes made by our players. I smiled as I remembered countless games in which I was the fan screaming at referees because they were disadvantaging my team. Moving from the referees, there were yells about the behavior of players on the opposing team. The other players were evil, whether through their actions that were obviously missed by the referees or for outright poor sportsmanship. I wasn't wearing those lenses so, to me, it all looked like a bunch of young men giving their all on the field.

The night did not go well for our team and the game was effectively over by the end of the first half. The opposing team decimated the offense, defense, and morale of our players in a fifteen-minute assault that left our crowd silent. I looked around and realized how much we all hate to lose.

If we choose to play, we're going to lose from time to time.

That is how it goes for us. If we choose to play, we're going to lose from time to time. The young men on that field last night will wake up today, lick their wounds, and move on. For many of them, last night will be the last time they ever play football. Their season has changed. For those of us who have experienced a few losses, we understand how it works. Sure, we may rage against the injustice of it—it is always safer for our sense of self if it is someone else's fault. But we move on. We let go. Because we know that if we don't, that anger, disappointment, and frustration sows doubt and negativity within us, ultimately lessening our joy and satisfaction in our own life.

Hating to lose doesn't go away, but we have to evolve. The only way to cope is to control our attitude, our reaction to our losses. When we fold or rage in the face of loss, we not only hurt our self, we hurt others around us because we drag them into it. When our anger and frustration spill over, it pollutes the very river on which we are traveling and everything else in it. The first mistake is to believe you will always win. The second is to anguish over the inevitable losses more than a moment. Life is far too precious. Time is far too fleeting.

Today, I awoke to a beautiful covering of frost on the ground. The sun was starting to appear, pasting its orange-yellow glow across the sky and illuminating the contrast of the green grass with the ghostly white frost. The vision filled me with a sense of joy for this new change. Another season appearing on the horizon full of possibility. I suppose I could sit here and lament the potential for losses that may come my way. But why? Sure, I still hate to lose. However, I choose to move toward the wins and trust that I'll find a way through when the bumps come.

Every Day Is Game Day

Each day you have the opportunity to pick yourself. Every day, you get into the game. Now is your chance. How will you play?

Show Up, Every Day

This is it! Your big chance to get in the game, your game. Alas, you can't play if you don't show up. Approaching every day like it's a game day requires us to be present for ourselves and for others. Our lives are collections of moments, and we need to be intentional if we are going to maximize them. Show up for yourself. Show up for others. Every day.

Own It, Every Day

Accountability. You cannot live your best life without it. Take responsibility for your existence by owning your decisions, and their consequences, every day. In similar fashion, avoid the temptation to blame others. When we blame others, we play small. We choose a lesser version of our self and allow someone else to set the tempo for our life. Even though we can't control the world around us, our choices remain ours. Own them every day.

Stand for Something, Every Day

Consider those you admire. Where do they stand? Then consider what they endure for that position. When we stand for something, we make it clear where our priorities lay. We take a position and share our beliefs. Taking a stand clarifies our thinking for our self and for others. Standing for something steels our resolve to believe. If we can't endure the criticism, can our belief be very strong? Find something worth standing for and stand for it every day.

Choose Happiness, Every Day

Happiness is a choice. I repeat: happiness is a choice. When we wait for something external to "make us happy," we relinquish responsibility and become a victim. Happiness is also a state of being, not a moment in time. Aspire to a joyful existence rather than fleeting gratifications. Choose to see the joy in your life and in the lives of others. Be grateful for what you have and enthusiastic for what's ahead. Choose happiness every day.

Give Your Best, Every Day

Giving your best is combination of effort and generosity. Your best effort is the greatest gift you can give to yourself and to others. Putting your all into an endeavor presents the risk of failure and the danger of exhaustion. It also offers the fulfillment and joy of playing at your peak. When we give our best, we call upon all of our unique faculties and elevate ourselves to something more. When we give our best, we bring others along with us. Give your best, every day.

Be Vulnerable, Every Day

We find vulnerability waiting for us at the edges—beyond which lie the best versions of our self. Vulnerability is a gateway through which we must pass to make the biggest difference in the world around us. When we show up, stand for something, and do our best, we make ourselves vulnerable. We must allow ourselves the grace of vulnerability if we ever hope to give the world the best version of our self. Be vulnerable, every day.

It's your life, your game, play it as only you can.

Acknowledgements

Thank you. Thank you for picking this book up. Thank you for walking this path with me. Thank you for taking the time to show up. For me, writing is casting my words into a big world with no expectation but to hope that they help someone in some way. Thank you for accepting a few of those words.

Thank you to Jon VanZile for sharing his editorial gifts with me and providing the delicate guidance necessary to help this author get to something he can be proud of. So glad to have teamed with you on book #2!

Thank you to my Northwind/Crosswind team. You are an amazing group of individuals and you inspire me to be better every day.

Thank you to my parents, Jerry and Trish, for setting me on a journey that has never failed to be an adventure and for providing loving examples that still move me to be the best version of myself.

Thank you to my wonderful family: Sally, Kiefer, Madison, Kellen, Macy, Ryan, Cooper, Jess, and Victoria. You give it all purpose. I am grateful to Madison for writing a wonderful Foreword and to Kellen for his modeling talents in the cover photo.

Thank you to the many wonderful people sharing their journeys with me and allowing me to share mine in turn. Your trials, triumphs, and friendship are priceless sources of inspiration. I am grateful for it all.

Other Sources of Inspiration

Leap First: Creating Work that Matters (Audiobook), Seth Godin, and pretty much everything else he's written

I Dare You!, William Danforth

Saving Private Ryan, DreamWorks, 1998

A Star is Born, Warner Brothers, 1976

The Matrix, Warner Brothers, 1999

Dead Poets Society, Buena Vista Pictures, 1989

Blink, Malcolm Gladwell

The Seven Habits of Highly Effective People, Stephen Covey

Daring Greatly, Brené Brown

"Freedom and Obligation – 2016 Commencement Address," Hillsdale College, Justice Clarence Thomas

Elon Musk: Tesla, SpaceX, and the Quest for a Fantastic Future, Ashlee Vance

About The Author

An accomplished business builder, Phillip Berry has built branch offices for national IT consulting firms, acquired, renovated, and sold an old General Motors factory building, built his own sales consulting practice, led business development for three startups, and facilitated more than a dozen acquisitions—including operations rolled into his four current businesses: Northwind Pharmaceuticals, Crosswind Pharmacy, Northwind Electronics, and Cross Stone Creative.

His latest venture, Christian Park Ventures, brings Phil's passion for redevelopment and community to the renovation of the former St. Bernadette's Church and School in the heart of Indianapolis. The renewed St. Bernadette's building will serve as headquarters for the Northwind/ Crosswind family of companies. Phil combines his leadership and entrepreneurial spirit with a sense of mission for the people, communities, and customers his businesses serve.

Phil's first book, *Stones Across the River: The Path to Your Best Work in Your Peak Years*, was published in 2016. Phil lives in Indianapolis, Indiana with his wife, Sally, where they raised four children (Kiefer, Madison, Kellen, and Macy), and now enjoy the company of their bulldog, Ripley, as well as visits from their first grandchild, Cooper.